W A N
H M O
O I T
?

Digital Identities, Cyber Troubles
and Legal Cures

Bob Seeman

ISBN: 9798377455769 (Hardcover)
ISBN: 9798377455240 (Paperback)

Cover design by: CyberCurb

Publisher: CyberCurb, Vancouver

About the Author

Bob Seeman is a Director of the Cyber Future Foundation Canada, an international collaboration of industry, public agencies and academia to build a more trusted and secure internet. Bob is a Mentor in the Rogers Cybersecure Catalyst, and an Entrepreneur-in-Residence at the Henri & Wolf cybersecurity law firm.

He advises boards of directors on cybersecurity and also cybersecurity companies that provide enterprise software.

Bob also has published *Ransomware Risk Mitigation for the Board*, and the foremost bitcoin-skeptic book, *The Coinmen*, which details how cryptocurrency is used for ransomware payments.

He is a California attorney, electrical engineer, and board director. Bob is a co-founder and former director of RIWI Corp., a public company that conducts data analytics, and has advised governments internationally on technology and business issues. Previously, he was Head of Strategy for Microsoft Network in London, and a technical consultant to the European Commission.

Bob previously practiced administrative law with an international law firm. He holds a Bachelor of Applied Science (Elec. Eng.) with Honours from the University of Toronto, a Master of Business Administration from EDHEC, and a Juris Doctor (J.D.) from the University of British Columbia.

For my friends.

Table of Contents

Digital Identity

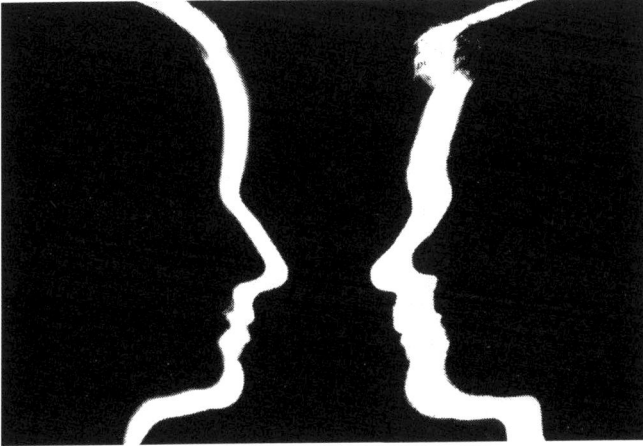

"Two guys meet each other in the middle of the street. One of them asks the other, 'Hey, aren't you the guy who always gets mistaken for someone else?' The other guy replies: 'No.'"

Introduction

The provision of most online services requires the user to have a unique digital identity. In order to receive such services conveniently and promptly, most people are willing to establish such an identity. However, a digital identity opens up many opportunities for mistakes, miscommunications, impersonations and other forms of fraud.

Juggling jurisdictional civil and criminal laws which evolve and change, risk assessment, human factors, online privacy, and threats from unknown adversaries makes protection of information systems integrity very challenging and costly to all organizations. This book introduces both the challenges and the methods by which these challenges can be met. It is a resource book that identifies the issues and points to solutions.

What is Digital Identity?

Digital identity is defined as the unique representation of a person when they engage in any online transaction. A person is, through their digital identity, allowed access to an online service and is identified as a user of that service. The person's uniqueness is based on specific attributes or identifiers.

Typically, proof of identity has been provided by, or on behalf of, governments. Proof of official identity generally depends on some form of government-provided or issued registration, documentation or certification, such as a birth certificate, identity card or national digital identity credential that provides attributes such as name, date and place of birth. There are new online identity models where digital credentials are provided by, or in partnership with, the private sector and recognised by governments as official proofs of online identity.

While a digital identity is always unique in the context of a digital service that does not mean that it uniquely identifies a person in all contexts. Moreover, a digital identity that is unique within the context of a digital service does not necessarily identify the real-life identity of the person.

Assessing and managing risks associated with digital identity systems includes processes such as identity proofing, authentication, and federation. The identity proofing process establishes that the identity belongs to a particular person. The digital authentication process establishes that someone attempting to access a digital service is the person with whom the service had previously dealt. The federation process allows for identity information to be shared in support of authentication across different systems and services.

For helpful definitions of terms found in this book, acronym meanings, and related words and phrases, please refer to the Digital Identity and Cybersecurity Dictionary.

"In God we trust, all others pay cash."

– Jean Shepherd, humorist and storyteller.

Cybersecurity and Privacy

Digital authentication provides privacy protection by mitigating the risk of unauthorized access to personal information. However, these functions can also create their own privacy and cybersecurity risks. Digital identity risk management efforts must always weigh cybersecurity, privacy, and usability issues one against the other to determine policy.

"Because he could not afford to fail, he could not afford to trust."

– Joseph Ellis, American historian.

Organizations must assess and manage digital identity cybersecurity risks such as unauthorized access, availability issues, impersonation, and other types of fraudulent claims. Organizations must consider potential impacts of security breaches on the confidentiality, integrity, and availability of information.

Digital identity systems, in their design and management, must be able to guarantee, to the best of their ability, privacy protection for all users who process personally identifiable information (PII).

"Never trust he who trusts everyone."

– Carlos Ruiz Zafón, the most widely published contemporary Spanish novelist.

Usability

Usability refers to human factors that impact on effectiveness, efficiency, and satisfaction of customers.

Usability requires an understanding of the goals and contexts of people interacting with a digital identity system. To provide an effective, efficient, and satisfactory experience for users, organizations need to consider the burden users face when entering the system and authenticating. Throughout the design and development lifecycle of a digital identity process, it is important to conduct usability evaluations with feedback from users on the challenges that they encounter when completing required tasks.

Digital identity management processes should be designed and implemented so it is easy and quick for users to do the right thing, hard to mess up, and uncomplicated to recover if and when mistakes are made.

"I trust no one, not even myself."

– Joseph Stalin, who knew himself well.

Parties

The parties involved in various digital identity functions are described below.

The Subject can be a) an Applicant applying for identity proofing, b) a Claimant waiting to be authenticated, and c) a Subscriber who has successfully completed the identity proofing process and the authentication.

A Credential Service Provider (CSP) is a trusted party whose functions include identity proofing Applicants and registering authenticated claimants to subscriber accounts. A subscriber account is the CSP's official record of the Subscriber, the Subscriber's attributes, and associated authenticators. A Relying Party (RP) is a party that relies upon the information in the subscriber account, typically to process a transaction or grant access to information or to an information system. A CSP need not be part of the RP, i.e. may be an independent third party.

A Verifier is a party whose function is to verify the Claimant's identity. This verification is done via an authentication protocol. To complete this, the Verifier needs to confirm the binding of the authenticators with the subscriber account and to check that the subscriber account is active.

The usual sequence of interactions for identity proofing and enrollment activities (non-federated) involves the following steps:

1. An Applicant applies to a CSP through an enrollment process. The CSP identity proofs that Applicant.
2. Upon successful proofing, the Applicant is enrolled in the identity service as a Subscriber. A subscriber account and corresponding authenticators (see section below) are established between the CSP and the Subscriber. The CSP maintains the

subscriber account, its status, and the enrollment data. The Subscriber maintains their authenticators.

3. The Relying Party (RP) requests authentication from the Claimant.
4. The Claimant proves possession and control of the authenticators to the Verifier through an authentication process (see section below). The Verifier interacts with the CSP to verify the binding of the Claimant's identity to their authenticators in the subscriber account and to optionally obtain additional Subscriber attributes. The CSP or Verifier functions of the service provider provide information about the Subscriber. The RP requests the attributes it requires from the CSP. The RP can use this information to make authorization decisions.
5. An authenticated session is established between the Subscriber and the RP.

"It is mutual trust, even more than mutual interest, that holds human associations together."

H. L. Mencken, American essayist, satirist.

Federated Model

A federated digital identity model benefits include:

- Enhanced user experience since a Subject can be identity proofed once and reuse the Subscriber account at multiple RPs.
- Cost reduction to both the Subject, due to a reduction in authenticators required, and the organization, due to reduction in information technology infrastructure.

- Minimizing data in applications since organizations do not need to collect, store, or dispose of personal information.
- Minimizing data exposed to applications by using pseudonymous identifiers and derived attribute values instead of copying account values to each application.
- Enabling organizations to focus on their core business without spending resources on identity management.

A federated model of authentication involves the following steps:

1. An Applicant applies to a federation protocol and Identity Provider (IdP) through an enrollment process. Using its CSP function, the IdP identity proofs the Applicant.
2. Upon successful proofing, the Applicant is enrolled in the identity service as a Subscriber. A subscriber account and corresponding authenticators are established between the IdP and the Subscriber. The IdP maintains the subscriber account, its status, and the enrollment data collected for, at minimum, the lifetime of the subscriber account. The Subscriber maintains their authenticators.
3. The RP requests authentication from the Claimant. The IdP provides an assertion and optionally additional attributes to the RP through a federation protocol.
4. The Claimant proves possession and control of the authenticators to the Verifier function of the IdP through an authentication process. Within the IdP, the Verifier and CSP functions interact to verify the binding of the Claimant's authenticators with those bound to the claimed subscriber account and may obtain additional Subscriber attributes.
5. All communication, including assertions, between the RP and the IdP occur through federation protocols.

6. The IdP provides the RP with the authentication status of the Subscriber and relevant attributes and an authenticated session is established between the Subscriber and the RP.

"The trust of the innocent is the liar's most useful tool."

– Stephen King, King of Horror.

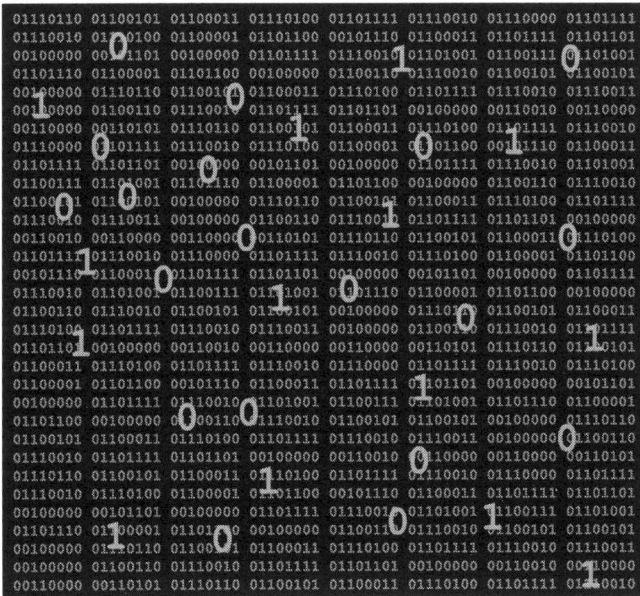

Authenticators

Authentication systems involves three factors as the cornerstones of authentication: something you know (e.g., a password), something you have (e.g., an ID badge or a cryptographic key), and something you are (e.g., a fingerprint or other biometric data).

Single-factor authentication requires only one of the above factors, most often "something you know." Multi-factor authentication (MFA) refers to the use of more than one distinct factor.

In digital authentication, the Claimant possesses and controls one or more authenticators (also known as Tokens). The authenticators will have been bound with the subscriber account. The authenticators contain secrets the Claimant can use to prove they are a legitimate subscriber. The Claimant authenticates to a system by demonstrating that they have possession and control of the authenticator. As explained above, once authenticated, the Claimant is referred to as a Subscriber.

The secrets contained in an authenticator are based on either key pairs (asymmetric cryptographic keys) or shared secrets (including symmetric cryptographic keys and memorized secrets). An asymmetric key pair involves both a public key and a related private key. The private key is stored on the authenticator and is only available for use by the Claimant who possesses and controls the authenticators. A Verifier that has the Subscriber's public key, for example through a public key certificate, can use an authentication protocol to verify that the Claimant has possession and control of the associated private key contained in the authenticators and, therefore, is a Subscriber.

While both keys and memorized secrets can be used in similar protocols, one important difference between the two is how they relate to the Claimant. Symmetric keys are generally chosen at random and are complex and long enough to thwart network-based guessing attacks, and stored in hardware or software that the Subscriber controls. Memorized secrets typically have fewer characters and less complexity than cryptographic keys to facilitate memorization and ease of entry. The result is that memorized secrets have increased vulnerabilities that require additional defenses to reduce the increased risk.

Authentication

A successful authentication process demonstrates that the Claimant has possession and control of one or more valid authenticators that are bound to the Subscriber's identity. In general, this authentication is done using an authentication protocol that involves an interaction between the Verifier and the Claimant. Well-designed protocols can protect the integrity and confidentiality of communication between the Claimant and the Verifier both during and after the authentication, and can help limit the damage that can be done by an attacker masquerading as a legitimate Verifier.

Additionally, mechanisms at the verifier stage can mitigate online guessing attacks against easier to guess secrets, such as passwords and PINs, by limiting the rate at which an attacker can make authentication attempts.

"Where large sums of money are concerned, it is advisable to trust nobody."

– Agatha Christie, mystery writer.

Initial Impact Assessment

An initial impact analysis identifies the potential adverse impacts of failures in identity proofing, authentication, and federation specific to an RP application or service, yielding an initial set of assurance levels.

The impact assessment includes: identifying impacted parties, identifying a set of impact categories for which harms will be assessed, identifying potential harms for each of the impact categories, identifying the levels of impact those potential harms would inflict should failures occur, and assessing the impact of each type of failure (proofing, authentication, and federation) and the resulting impact level on all affected parties.

When assessing impacts, an organization needs to determine the parties, especially the individuals, that will be impacted.

Initial assurance levels for digital transactions are determined by assessing the potential impact of: damage to mission delivery, damage to trust or reputation, loss of sensitive information, damage to or loss of economic stability, loss of life or damage to safety, health, or environmental stability, noncompliance with laws, regulations, and contractual obligations.

Initial assurance levels for digital transactions are determined by assessing the potential impact of a failure: low potential impact could be expected to have a limited adverse effect; moderate potential impact could be expected to have a serious adverse effect; and, high potential impact could be expected to have a severe or catastrophic adverse effect.

An impact analysis helps to determine the extent to which risk must be mitigated by the identity proofing, authentication, and federation processes. These determinations drive the relevant of applicable technologies and mitigation strategies.

3758191069916904123820453764375819106 9
91697567202047984804123820453764431876
18771914756720204798482592875196208643
18761877191422572855401062259287519620
86659969066388402257285540106273524785
69606965999690663884041397461533720735 2
47856960696832687109834441397461533720
5132358253520568326871098344612433937 0
01295132358253520507108153949758612433
93700129448471300710815349975864847130
375819106991693012382036758191069916 94
4574000988412382075672247445376443187 6
18771917567202047984843187618977191 25
2875196208642592875196208622572855401 0
6269969066388022572855401062546386960 6
9599690663884075247536373524197415372 0
478569606968341397461533720268710983 44
68326871098351323582535205446513235825
35205124339370012960121081539984339370
012974750847130710815394975844484713 0
3758191069916904 23820453764375819106 9
91697567202047984804123820 537644318 76
187 191475672020479848259287519620864 3
18761877191 2257 8554 106 59287519620
8665 969066 8 4 2572 5540 06273 24785
  960696 99   0663   4   41397   153   720735
47 56 606 6   3 68 10 83 44   97   1 3   720
51 23582535 05 8 2 871098   461 4339370
01   9   32   3 2 5071 8 5   497 8 124 3
     1 9448   713   71   1539   7 8 484713
37 8191 69   6 30 2382   67   191 6991   94
4   40 09   2382   5 7 247   537 44 1 7
18   1 17567   04 98484431   61   7719 25
8 51 6   86 25 2 751   2   2 7 8554 1
62   9 90663 8   2   28 5401   2 4 8   06
95 9   0   3   5 4   6 7   4 9 415   2
  7   6   0 96   41   7 6 5 3   68 1   4
68 26 7   98 5132 582 35 0   465   2   25
    05 24 3   70 1 96   1 8   3 9 4 3

Identity Verification

Identity verification verifies that the claimed identity is associated with the real-life person supplying the identity evidence. The goal of identity verification is to confirm and establish a linkage between the claimed identity and the real-life existence of the Applicant engaged in the identity proofing process.

The CSP can verify the linkage of the claimed identity to the Applicant engaged in the identity proofing process through one or more of the following methods:

- Enrollment code verification.

- In-person physical comparison. The CSP operator and Applicant interact in person for the identity proofing event. The CSP operator does a physical comparison of the face on the photo presented on identity evidence to the face of the Applicant engaged in the identity proofing event.
- Remote (attended and unattended) physical facial image comparison. The CSP operator performs a physical comparison of the facial portrait presented on identity evidence to the facial image of the Applicant engaged in the identity proofing event.
- Automated biometric comparison. Biometric system comparison may be performed for in-person or remote identity proofing events. The facial portrait, or other biometric characteristic, contained on identity evidence is compared by an automated biometric comparison system to the facial image photograph of the live Applicant or other biometric live sample submitted by the Applicant during the identity proofing event.
- Control of a digital account. A person is able to demonstrate control of a digital account, such as a online bank account, or signed digital assertion through the use of authentication or federation protocols. This authentication may be performed in person through presentation of the credential to a device or reader, or during remote identity proofing sessions.

Threats and Security Considerations

Effective protection of identity proofing processes requires the layering of security controls throughout a transaction. The main threats to the identity proofing process are:

- Impersonation – where an attacker attempts to pose as someone else (e.g., identity theft).
- False or fraudulent representation – where an attacker may create a false identity or false claims

about an identity, such as synthetic identity fraud. Synthetic identity theft is a special form of fraud in which a Social Security number (SSN) is stolen (or purchased on the Dark Web) and then a name, date of birth, mailing address, email account and phone number are made up and applied to that legitimate SSN to create a new identity.

- Infrastructure — where attackers may seek to compromise confidentiality, integrity and availability of the infrastructure, data, software, or people supporting the CSPs identity proofing process, such as a distributed denial of service attack.

Conclusion

Digital identity solutions are of prime importance to business and service functions. Close coordination of identity functions with cybersecurity teams, threat intelligence teams, and program integrity teams can improve and maintain business protection.

Risk Assessment, Management and Governance

"They've finally come up with the perfect office computer. If it makes a mistake, it blames another computer."

– Milton Berle, an American actor and comedian.

Introduction

The growth of and increased reliance on digital identity highlights the importance of cybersecurity risk assessment and management in all large organizations and, increasingly, in small businesses. With the reality of billions of connected digital devices, the potential impact of a cyberattack or disruption to digital infrastructure can become a matter of major significance. It is crucial that all organizations and, in fact, all individuals, understand and actively participate in assessing and managing these risks.

Risk Assessment

Risk assessment has three components: (1) identification and estimation of degree of hazard, (2) assessment of the company's exposure and vulnerability, and (3) estimation of risk by combining likelihood of occurrence and severity of outcome.

"When the inventor of the drawing board messed things up, what did he go back to?"

– Bob Monkhouse, an English comedian.

Risk Management

Risk management involves evaluating the information obtained from risk assessments and, based on this information, making decisions about which risks are acceptable, tolerable, or intolerable. The choices for managing risk may include mitigation, transfer (i.e. transferring the risk to another party by agreement with that party and/or obtaining insurance), or sharing of risk meaning that no one person bears the brunt (i.e. the cost of remediation.) Choices will depend on what has been called an organization's "risk appetite".

Four types of risk have been identified, each one requiring different risk management plans: routine risks, complex risks, uncertain risks, and ambiguous risks. Specific approaches to management of risk include a statistical analysis for routine risks, a cost-benefit analysis for complex risks, a precautionary approach for uncertain risks, and participatory decision-making for ambiguous risks.

The public perception of risk often differs from actual risk due to common cognitive biases such as a tendency to exaggerate dreaded risks that are rare and downplaying commonplace risks that are, indeed, common. It is important to align public perception with actual risk. Risk-benefit analysis is important.

Another way of structuring risk assessment is to consider the four core concepts of vulnerability, threat, likelihood, and impact. Vulnerability is an inherent weakness in a system that can easily lead to an undesirable outcome if it is exploited. Threat is the would-be exploit (cyberattack) by an attacker. Likelihood is the estimated probability that a threat will exploit a vulnerability, and impact is the negative effect of that happening.

"Good judgment comes from experience, and experience comes from bad judgment."

– Rita Mae Brown, an American feminist writer.

Risk Governance

Risk governance is vital. It helps organizations make informed decisions regarding the potential risks that they face and how to manage them both before and after they occur. The initial process of risk governance involves a thorough examination of the context (how often and against whom are cyberattacks occurring), assessing risks and concerns (sophistication of employees, training of employees), characterizing those risks (identifying them and communicating them), managing them, and continually monitoring and refining the process to ensure that it is effective and current. The principles of risk governance ensure that decisions are made based on a clear understanding of the legal, social, organizational, and economic context, all of which changes with time.

A structured process of risk management is required, not random decisions that rely on intuition and bias. All employees must understand cyber risk. Training, behavior change, trust building, and stakeholder involvement are crucial. Rules about security routines, password complexity, confidentiality and frequent adjustment are bothersome for employees. Rather than being imposed, they need to be explained, discussed and willingly accepted. Every employee must ultimately be accountable for failure to accept regulations. Training needs to be reviewed, improved, and repeated. Ideally, failures in the risk governance process should lead to constant feedback and improvement. Individuals need to be able to freely report accidental policy breaches so that they can be corrected.

Some organizations tend toward technocratic risk management that is based on scientific evidence; some choose a decisionistic style that incorporates social and economic drivers of risk; and some organizations are more transparent than others, meaning that their decisions are based on input from stakeholders and are known to all stakeholders. The key to successful risk governance is to ensure that it is tightly coupled with day-to-day decision-making, such as health and safety, finances, and human resources. The cyber risk governance approach should be part of the operational culture of the company and be wholeheartedly adopted by everyone involved. The more inclusive and transparent the policy development, the more likely it will receive support and buy-in from stakeholders.

"Whoever is careless with the truth in small matters cannot be trusted with important matters."

– Albert Einstein, an absent minded genius. Many quotes attributed to Einstein are apocryphal.

Human Factors and Risk Communication

Human factors such as employees not understanding the importance of confidential data and system security, not perceiving that they are at risk, and not following safe policies can and do impact security governance. Risk communication is crucial in addressing these challenges. It means involvement of all stakeholders, education, creating confidence that permits behaviour change, and leading by example. What needs to be communicated is a sense of responsibility and accountability in a culturally-sensitive and morally ethical context. For further detail, see the Human Factors chapter in this book.

It is important to create a company culture where people feel comfortable reporting issues and concerns, without fear of being penalized. Security works for everyone. It's important to note that completing awareness training does not always guarantee that graduates will comply with regulations. It is human to slip up or to be unknowingly taken in by guile.

NIST Risk Assessment Guidelines

The US Government's National Institute of Standards and Technology (NIST) risk assessment guidelines capture the vulnerability, threats, likelihood and impact elements within what they refer to as the Prepare, Conduct, Communicate, and Maintain cycle:

- Prepare: Defining the purpose, scope, and assumptions for the assessment, as well as identifying sources of information about threats, vulnerabilities, and impact. Preparing also means determining the assessment approach to take and the amount of risk tolerance one is willing to assume.
- Conduct: Carrying out the assessment, analyzing the information, documenting the results and communicating them to stakeholders.
- Communicate: Determining who needs to be informed, what information needs to be shared, how it will be communicated, and communicating it. It also means obtaining feedback and incorporating it into the risk management process.
- Maintain: Continuous monitoring and updating of the risk assessment so that it reflects changes in the environment or context. Reassessment may be necessary. Also necessary is verifying that the risk management plan is being implemented effectively, and making changes whenever needed.

Vulnerability Management

The vulnerability of software is important to assess and re-assess regularly. Automated tools can scan the network to identify vulnerable assets and generate reports that should be reviewed regularly to prioritize and schedule fixes. Factors like impact, visibility, and ease of exploitation need to be considered when prioritizing fixes.

The distinction between security and safety is important in the context of cyber-physical systems and the hardware and software systems used to operate industrial control devices (operational technology or OT.) While traditional IT security focuses on minimizing access, modification, and downtime within components and systems, OT risks demand focus on safety due to the impact of failure on worker and public safety. To mitigate these risks, a systems-driven approach to risk management is recommended, with the focus on high-level objectives such as avoiding harm and complying with regulations.

Security Metrics

There are open questions about what features of a system to measure for security, how to measure them, and why they need to be measured. Good metrics should be easy and inexpensive to measure, expressed with cardinal numbers and familiar units, and relevant to one's business. Qualitative ratings such as high/medium/low are best avoided.

Incident Management

Incident management is a crucial aspect of cybersecurity and risk assessment, management, and governance. Incident management involves responding to cyberattacks, minimizing their impact, implementing a remediation plan, and using the lessons learned to improve defenses and plan for the future.

Information Sharing with Other Organizations

Sharing information about cybersecurity breaches, while still considered taboo in many organizations, is becoming increasingly important as offenders increasingly collaborate and share intelligence about opportunities and vulnerabilities. Many industries, such as the financial and pharmaceutical sectors, have established information-sharing arrangements.

"There are worse things than getting a call for a wrong number at 4 am. It could be a right number."

– Doug Larson, a columnist.

Conclusion

Proper cybersecurity and digital identity risk assessment and management will reduce the risk of cyberattacks and disruption to digital infrastructure, including digital identity infrastructure. The principles laid out in this chapter, when followed, should reduce successful cyberattacks and, should they occur, reduce the negative outcomes.

Human Factors

*"To make a mistake is human,
but to blame it on someone else,
that's even more human."*

Introduction

The principles for designing reliable digital identity and cybersecurity are rooted in a knowledge of human behavioral sciences – psychology, forensics, and economics. We have learned that secure communication systems need to be user-friendly and not impose excessive cognitive burden on users. The number of security measures that a person or an organization needs to take have to be minimized as much as possible. The effort required to bypass a security measure should be substantially greater than the resources and potential rewards for the cyberattacker.

The failure of cybersecurity measures is not attributable to users being, as often said, the "weakest link". Rather, the failure lies in the security design that ignored factors such as usability and acceptability. Password policies highlight this issue. Research has shown that policies designed by security experts are often bypassed by employees and, thus, ineffective. Software developers also put in outdated mechanisms that have proven faulty. Findings such as these emphasize the need for a focus on human factors in the design and implementation of secure systems.

When users do not follow security policies, they are blamed for not understanding the risks or simply being too lazy. But non-compliance or "rule-bending" is just as often a result of a "Sophie's choice" (A choice where both alternatives carry negative consequences) between productivity and security, and choosing productivity because that is the more immediate organizational demand.

The typical response to non-compliance is security awareness and education, but this approach is not always effective. Human factors research has established that "fitting the task to the human" is more efficient than the other way around in terms of both cost and performance. Security awareness and training can play a role in improving security, but it should not be the first resort. Security must be usable, with usability being defined as the effectiveness, efficiency, and satisfaction of users achieving their goals. Security must work for people.

Usability

Criteria for assessing the usability of a system are:

- Effectiveness: The accuracy and completeness with which specified users can achieve their goals in a specific context.
- Efficiency: The resources (e.g. time and effort) expended in relation to the accuracy and completeness of the goals that one tries to achieve.
- Satisfaction: The comfort and acceptability of the system to its users and those affected by its use. It is a measure of the user's level of enjoyment and ease with the task.
- Capabilities and limitations of target users: Understanding the skills, knowledge, and abilities of users is crucial in designing security measures that are within their easy reach. Security measures should align with the other goals and tasks that users need to perform routinely.
- Physical and social context: The context puts constraints on the ease of performing security tasks.
- The capabilities and limitations of the device: The device on which security measures are used can also play a role in their usability, e.g. screen size, processing power, and input methods.

Humans have general physical and mental capabilities and limitations, and tasks that exceed these capabilities will not succeed. Security mechanisms must not demand too much time or attention, and should be clearly and simply placed in front of the user to require a response, not be reliant on a user's memory.

Alarm Fatigue

Alarm fatigue refers to a situation where users stop paying attention to security warnings due to the relatively high rate of false alarms. This situation is like the boy who cries "wolf", when the brain begins to classify repeated signals as irrelevant and filters them out before they reach consciousness. To avoid alarm fatigue, it is important to keep the alarm rate as low as possible and to only issue security warnings when necessary. At the time of issuing a security warning, explain why it is important and precisely what needs doing. The recommendation is to keep the false alarm rate below 10%. Above that percentage, it loses its effect. Suggested ways of doing this includes good technology support. Job rotation is also a good idea, although it is not always possible. With human beings, being what they are, once they begin dismissing alarms, it becomes difficult to turn the clock backward.

"Anyone who has never made a mistake has never tried anything new."

– Albert Einstein, one of the greatest and most influential physicists of all time.

Human Memory

Memory is a key mental capability in humans and is divided into short-term memory (STM) and long-term memory (LTM). STM is used for temporary storage of information, like one-time passwords, but it has limited capacity and can only easily handle strings of up to 6 characters. Long-term memory is divided into semantic memory (LTM-SM) and episodic memory (LTM-EM.) The ability to recall information stored in LTM depends on how frequently it is retrieved. Infrequently used information stored in LTM-SM fades faster than information stored in LTM-EM because the latter is connected to personal history and emotions. Overloading the STM loop with long or alpha-numeric codes takes more time and has a greater likelihood of error.

To better cope with the memory issue, the following solutions are recommended: multi-factor authentication, password managers, or keeping strong passwords for longer periods.

Passwords

A knowledge-based authentication credential, such as a password, needs to be extremely difficult to guess.

Easier guesses for attackers:

- Users usually pick passwords that are easy for them to recall, such as personally significant names or dates.
- When using images as credentials, users usually prefer stronger colours and shapes.
- When the images are pictures of humans, they will choose more attractive people.
- When using a location within a picture, people prefer obvious features.
- With a location-based system, people pick memorable locations; when choosing locations for a 4-digit PIN on a number grid, they choose locations on the grid that are next to each other and at an edge or corner of the grid.
- The order of the elements (e.g. letters, numbers, characters) of a credential is predictable. People who write languages that read left-to-right will choose the elements in that order.
- With finger swipe passwords, users generally choose from a limited number of shapes.

These biases in the selection of credentials result in easily guessable knowledge-based authentication, making it less secure. To reduce this risk, security systems can implement various measures such as randomizing the order of elements, offering a wide range of options to choose from, or using multiple elements to form a single credential. These changes increase the randomness of the system, making it more secure against guessing attacks.

Security policies have also restricted too obvious password choices, but these polices have increased the workload associated with password creation and recall, causing frustration and time lost in retrieval. Visible password strength "meters" have been used to guide password choices, but these meters can vary in accuracy. The workload associated with password creation can also increase with restrictions, and password strength meters. It is also important to consider the specific needs of different user groups, such as children, older citizens, and those with physical and mental conditions. The usability limitations of security mechanisms and their contribution to security fatigue must also be kept in mind.

"Whenever I struggle with my identity, I go to the bathroom and look in the mirror."

User Behaviour

Workarounds to security measures, like writing down passwords, occur because people want to ensure effective completion of their tasks and protect business productivity. The repeated effort and disruption of entering a password many times a day can lead to negative effects such as installing mouse-jiggling software to avoid screen lock.

The aim must be to reduce the burden of security tasks on users. This can be done by automating security, minimizing the need for explicit human action, triggering security mechanisms only when necessary, and designing systems that are secure by default. As people tend to prefer physical tasks over mental tasks, the design should aim to reduce mental workload as much as possible.

To reduce security compliance fatigue, security specialists need to discuss with line managers and business leaders the time and budget available for security tasks. Making security mechanisms smarter and less restrictive reduce compliance fatigue. Access to efficient security recovery and support services reduces the need for workarounds.

Multi-factor authentication solutions, despite providing better security, may still be difficult for users to use if they are hard to handle, or require users to carry authenticators (tokens). These usability issues can lead to confusion and human error, reducing their effectiveness.

The majority of activities that people undertake are carried out in a fast and automatic mode, making people efficient but also making them vulnerable to security risks. It is unrealistic to expect people to always be cautious when they have numerous work emails with embedded links that may need to be clicked on. Productivity is threatened if they cannot complete their primary task without clicking on these links. Users must be educated as to the need for complex additional tasks and given options.

Factors such as fatigue, inexperience, and risk-taking attitude can lead to errors. Human factors such as memory limitations and shared assumptions also contribute. Factors such as time pressure, high workload, monotony, and boredom can lead to errors, as well as uncertainty about roles, responsibilities and rules. Work environment factors such as interruptions and poor equipment and lack of information can also cause errors, particularly when rules and procedures change. The responsibility to address these factors lies with the organization and regular reviews should be conducted to identify and address underlying causes of mistakes and near misses.

Security Awareness Education and Training

Security awareness education helps people understand what the cybersecurity risks are and what they can do to reduce them. The emphasis is on why security matters, what it means for the organisation, and what it means for the individual. Education should be targeted and tailored to its audience, delivered in a way that is easy to understand and relevant. It should also be engaging, interactive and provide practical advice on how to reduce the risk.

Security training equips people with the skills that they need to reduce risk. Training should be focused on the tasks that people need to perform in order to be safe. It helps people acquire skills, such as how to use a security mechanism correctly or recognize and respond to a social engineering attack (e.g., a con artist). Training is more effective when it takes place in a social community and allows people to practice the skills and discuss their perceptions and biases. It should be practical, hands-on training that provides opportunities for people to practice what they have learned. It is also important that training be regularly reviewed and updated to keep pace with new risks and changing threats.

Simulations and games are often used to make security awareness more appealing and to support more comprehensive education and behavioral change. Anti-phishing simulations, which teach employees not to click on suspicious links in emails or elsewhere, are the most widely used in organizations. These simulations measure the impact of interventions and show a decrease in click rates in the short term. However, the success of these simulations depends on the employee's motivation to engage in the training and their ability to apply the skills being taught. Anti-phishing simulations can also have negative effects, such as reducing trust among employees or leading to reluctance to click on any links, including important ones. Designing simulations must take this issue into account. Using email filtering solutions can effectively reduce the number of suspicious emails.

Security education and training should be an integral part of an overall security strategy. They should be integrated with other security measures, such as technical controls and policies, to provide a comprehensive security solution. The key is to balance the need for security with the need for people to be able to complete their tasks efficiently and effectively.

"How would you like a job where, when you made a mistake, a big red light goes on and 18,000 people boo?"

– Jacques Plante, an ice hockey goaltender.

Security Policies

General MacArthur's statement to "never give an order that can't be obeyed" applies to security policies as well. When employees encounter security policies that are impossible or extremely difficult to follow or are clearly not effective, it undermines the credibility of all policies and the security professionals who issue them. If policies are not being followed, security professionals must investigate why this is the case and re-design the solution. In most cases, employees do not mean to show blatant disregard for security. They are usually trying to manage a risk that they understand in the best way they know how.

To make security a credible proposition, it must be framed as a positive aspect that enables people to engage in activities that they value and to experience positive outcomes. Key aspects of such "positive security" policy is to emphasize such positive outcomes and not blame those who are unable to follow security advice. This positive conception of security encourages individuals to become more involved in both decision-making and behaving securely.

Conclusion

The ultimate goal of cybersecurity is to protect people, their information, and their digital identity. The design of digital identity and cybersecurity mechanisms must take into account the capabilities and limitations of human users and strive to fit the task to the human – rather than the other way around.

Privacy

"My bank must stop trying to sell me identity theft protection. You know why I expect you to protect my money? Because you're a bank."

— Bill Maher, Comedian.

Introduction

In today's world, private individual's data and digital identity are being collected, processed, and disseminated far and wide to persons unknown. The potential harms of such widespread use of private information due to a cybersecurity or digital identity breach range from physical or psychological damage to

49

individuals, to political and economic impacts. Privacy is not only about confidentiality. It includes issues such as democratic values, freedom of speech and individual autonomy.

This chapter discusses systems that will protect users' privacy. It covers the identification of privacy problems, their technical description, and technologies that eliminate, or at least mitigate, those problems.

The primary goals of privacy-preserving systems are to increase trust and minimize risk. These goals are achieved by disclosing as little as possible, collecting as little as possible, minimizing the replication and retention of data, cutting down on linkages between data, and avoiding centralization of data. Strategies such as these constrain the flow of information to parties other than those intended to receive it. Thus, the strategies limit the number of places where data is stored or processed, avoids a single point of potential fraudulent or adversarial attack, and limits the amount of time that the information is stored.

While still allowing information exchange, privacy technologies implement these strategies and preserve the integrity of the system. The first step in choosing a privacy technology is to identify the data flows that need to be minimized, and the minimum amount of information that needs to be transferred. Minimizing information flow includes keeping data within a firewall, encrypting the data, using cryptography, obfuscating, or anonymizing the data.

There are two main approaches to achieving data privacy. The first is data confidentiality (using confidentiality technologies), which focuses on preventing unauthorized access. This approach is typically achieved through the use of cryptography. The second approach is disclosure control (using control technologies), which involves both limiting the amount of information that is able to be leaked to the adversary, and ensuring, to the extent possible, that any leaked data cannot be linked to any specific individual.

"Don't trust people who tell you other people's secrets."

– Dan Howell, an English YouTube comedian.

Confidentiality Technologies

Cryptography includes end-to-end encryption (E2EE) and Off-the-Record Messaging (OTR). E2EE protects the confidentiality of data in transit between the sender and recipient, while also ensuring integrity and authentication. In E2EE, the encryption keys are held by the devices at the end of the communication, which can be agreed upon using key transport or Diffie-Hellman exchange. This is a mathematical method of securely exchanging cryptographic keys over a public channel. OTR, on the other hand, strengthens privacy properties and considers an adversary who can observe and compromise the devices involved in communication.

As with most anything else, approaches such as cryptography come with trade-offs. They involve high resource requirements, and are characterized by low efficiency, and limited flexibility. There are alternative methods of obfuscating data that are less effective but more efficient. These methods control the amount of information that can be inferred from a data set. How well that works depends on the nature of the data and cleverness of the unintended receiver. The privacy gained from these techniques is based on limiting the available information, which may, of course, impact on its utility.

Anonymization is a technique used to process data without risking individual privacy. It separates identity from information by removing names or other identifiers. This makes the data unlinkable and lessens a reader's ability to make inferences about its meaning or importance. However, full anonymity is difficult to achieve as most data contain enough information to correlate different attributes and/or records in a database. Unique data patterns, called quasi-identifiers, can be used to re-identify individuals. To limit the risk of re-identification, anonymization is often combined with other obfuscation techniques such as generalization and suppression.

Generalization is a technique that reduces the precision of data by using ranges or statistics (such as an average), for example, instead of specific numbers.

Suppression is a technique that involves hiding part of the information. The idea is that the fewer data that are available, the more difficult it is to make inferences. For instance, instead of "Mary made a million dollars," the message instead states "One of the employees won an exceptional prize." The best privacy results can be obtained by using suppression strategies that are tailored to the nature and characteristics of the data but that can only be understood by a reader with prior knowledge of the topic at hand.

Metadata

Metadata are data about data. Examples are traffic metadata, device metadata, and location metadata.

Traffic metadata include information about the communication infrastructure such as identities of participants, data transfer amount and timing, and duration of connection. Metadata of this sort can be used to infer sensitive information about individuals or companies. Anonymous communication networks can protect against this risk. Such networks are formed by relays that change the appearance of messages through encryption and alter the traffic patterns.

Device metadata are associated with the platform generating the data and can, thus, reveal sensitive information about the device and its owner. To protect against this, various privacy-enhancing technologies such as Virtual Private Networks (VPNs), Tor, or encrypting device data can be used. Device metadata include specific characteristics of a user's device, such as browser type and version, screen resolution, installed fonts, that are often sent along with data requests in order to optimize the service provider's response. The information can be used to identify and track users, even if they are anonymous on the network layer. This process is called browser or device fingerprinting, which makes it possible for service providers to track users across the web. Defending against device metadata attacks is difficult, as hiding this information from online service providers affects device performance.

Location metadata are associated with the physical location from which data are generated. It reveals potentially sensitive information about an individual's location and activities. There are ways to protect against this by using a GPS spoofer or disabling location services on the devices that one uses.

Tor Network

Tor is the most popular anonymous communication network. It uses "onion" encryption to protect user's privacy by routing traffic through a series of Onion Routers (ORs). When a user wants to access a service, they install a Tor browser on their device. The browser builds a circuit of three ORs (entry, middle, and exit nodes) and routes encrypted traffic to the destination server through that circuit. A secret key is established with each of the ORs in the circuit and encrypts the packet in layers before it is sent to the destination server. The server sends data back in reverse order, i.e. the server encrypts the message in layers that are decrypted by exit, middle, and entry ORs. ORs do not purposely impose delays on messages, so that traffic patterns are conserved. This means that an attacker could link the origin and destination of communication by seeing both ends of the communication. Mix networks exist that protect against attacks by delaying messages or adding new real or dummy messages to the mix.

The difference between Tor and a VPN is that Tor is decentralized so that no single relay can learn the link between the sender and receiver. A VPN is centralized, meaning that a VPN provider can read the correspondence between the sender and receiver.

"I changed my password to 'incorrect', so anytime I forget and enter the wrong thing, the computer tells me what it is."

Control Technologies

As opposed to simply keeping messages confidential, privacy technologies provide control over personal information. In many cases, revealing data may be necessary or perceived as beneficial, but it is important to consider the control over how the data is used. The privacy as control paradigm addresses two main concerns: 1) allowing users to express their preferences for data use, and 2) allowing organizations to define and enforce policies to prevent misuse of the data.

Democratic Values

Privacy protection is crucial for valued activities such as electronic voting. Electronic voting systems are designed to provide a secure and trustworthy environment for casting votes. They use encryption and digital signatures to ensure that votes are kept confidential, and that the voting process is tamper-proof. They also use privacy-preserving techniques such as homomorphic encryption and zero-knowledge proofs to hide the content of individual votes while still allowing them to be counted.

Electronic petitions that allow citizens to express their opinions and call for change by signing an online petition are done through a dedicated website, or through social media platforms. They also use privacy technologies such as encryption and digital signatures to protect users' identities and to prevent manipulation.

Censorship systems aim to control the distribution of content by preventing users from publishing or accessing certain content. Privacy-preserving technologies play a crucial role in supporting freedom of speech and access to information by making censorship resistance possible. For example, the Freenet system uses encryption and anonymous authentication to protect the publishing of content on the Internet and make selective denial of service and coercion by law enforcement difficult. Freenet is a peer-to-peer system that allows for the publication, replication, and retrieval of data while protecting the anonymity of both authors and readers. It also uses keys to locate files and prevent the identity of the recipient from being knowable. The random accessing of information by various parts of the network also provide deniability and protect anonymity.

Tangler is a censorship-resistant application. It splits files into small blocks that are stored on different servers. In order to retrieve a file, multiple servers must be contacted to obtain all the necessary blocks. It replicates entangled files, making it difficult for a censor to delete a target file. Censorship-resistant data access can be achieved through mimicking, tunnelling, embedding communication within other content, and hiding its destination. Mimicking means making censored data look allowable. Tunnelling "tunnels within" popular data services to transmit the censored communication, making it difficult for censors to block. Embedding communication within other content makes it hard to find and deniable. Hiding the destination of communication involves relaying censored traffic through intermediate parts of the network and disguising the connections.

"If I'm not telling you something, it's for a reason. Just because you trust me, it doesn't mean I have to automatically trust you. Trust doesn't work like that."

– David Levithan, young adult fiction writer.

Conclusion

There are many cybersecurity methods to protect private data and digital identity from disclosure or censorship but also many ways of countering cybersecurity systems. Methods are always changing and becoming increasingly sophisticated. To stay ahead of the curve and protect the organization and the privacy and digital identity of individuals who share information with the organization, it is important hire, retain and continually train a top team of professionals to deploy appropriate cybersecurity and digital identity confidentiality and control technologies.

Law and Regulation

"When I was a kid, my mother told me I could be anyone I wanted to be.

Turns out, identity theft is a crime."

Introduction

Understanding "the law" helps business people know when to call in their lawyers, how to interpret their legal advice and how to value their contributions. This chapter is intended to provide an introduction to business people of laws and regulations relevant to cybersecurity, privacy and digital identity.

Legal risk management involves understanding the laws and regulations that apply in all the jurisdictions in which the business operates. It means the ability to assess the legal and enforcement risks that business can incur. Assessment is a challenging task due to the large number of laws and regulations, varying laws and enforcement authority across multiple jurisdictions, and the complexities of private law and regulatory systems.

Laws are created by the legislative authority, interpreted by the judicial authority, and enforced by the executive authority. Laws can be in the form of primary legislation, such as an Act of Congress, or secondary legislation where law-making authority is delegated to other regulatory agencies because of their technical expertise.

Civil Law

Civil law governs private relationships between individuals. It deals with issues such as contracts, property rights, and torts (dealing with issues such as negligence). In contrast to criminal law, the focus of civil law is on compensation rather than punishment. Should a person breach a civil law that harms another person, the latter can sue. Civil law remedies include compensation, termination of a legal relationship, an injunction to stop harmful activities, or an order to take specific actions. In the context of cybersecurity, civil law deals with issues related to poor security practices in the development of information and communication technology products and services.

"A nosy identity thief is the absolute worst.

He has that annoying habit of making other peoples lives his own."

Criminal Law

Criminal law governs behavior considered unacceptable by society. It is enforced by the state to deter bad behaviour, limit the ability of a criminal to cause harm, seek retribution for crime committed, compensate the victim, and (at least in theory) rehabilitate the criminal. The terms "guilty" and "innocent" are reserved for verdicts in criminal cases.

Punishments include imprisonment, fines, forfeiture of criminal proceeds, and restitution to the victim.

Proof and Evidence

The concept of "proof" in law refers to using permissible evidence to demonstrate the truth of events that are contested. Evidence can take various forms, such as witness testimony, business records, recordings, and photographs.

The standard of proof in law is the level of certainty required to demonstrate the truth of contested events. The standard varies depending on the type of legal matter, with criminal cases generally requiring a higher degree of certainty (beyond a reasonable doubt) compared to civil cases (balance of probabilities). The standard of proof must be met by the party carrying the burden of proof (generally the government in criminal matters or the person starting the legal proceedings in civil matters), who must use admissible evidence to prove their case to the finder of fact (e.g. judge, jury, or regulator).

Legal risk analysis often includes consideration of the rules and the relative ability of each party to prove their case. Therefore, documentation is necessary to prove one's case. Document retention policies are important to businesses. If a legal action is threatened, destruction of relevant evidence is illegal.

Jurisdiction

Jurisdiction refers to the authority of a state to assert legal power over entities operating within its literal and online territory. The principles of "conflict of laws" determines which law applies to resolve disputes that cross jurisdictional borders. The rise of online activities has led to an increase in cross-border legal responsibilities, making it important to consider jurisdiction and conflict of law principles.

There are three aspects of jurisdiction to consider: prescriptive jurisdiction, juridical jurisdiction, and enforcement jurisdiction. Prescriptive jurisdiction refers to the scope of a state's authority to make laws and regulate activities. Juridical jurisdiction refers to a court's authority to make decisions in a case. Enforcement jurisdiction refers to a state's ability to enforce its laws, including through arrest, or court order such as seizure of property. These concepts apply to multi-state activities conducted online.

States can claim prescriptive jurisdiction over non-resident persons who solicit business from residents or over actions taken by their own nationals while outside its borders. There may be cases where more than one state claims jurisdiction over a single act.

States assert prescriptive and juridical jurisdiction over actions that harm their residents, whether these actions take place within or outside of the state's territory. In the case of actions taking place outside of the state's territory, courts may interpret domestic law in a way that asserts jurisdiction if the content is visible to persons within the state. Examples of laws enforced in this manner include copyright, defamation, and gambling. This practice of asserting jurisdiction is based on the state's interest in protecting its residents and its domestic market.

States with computer crime laws often have jurisdiction over actions that target computers located within their territory, even if the person committing the action is located outside of the state. Cyberattackers who conduct offensive activity against computers located in another state are responsible if they violate the criminal law of that state, even if the activity is not illegal in the state where the cyberattacker is physically present.

The General Data Protection Regulation (GDPR) in the European Union (EU), brought a significant change to the territorial prescriptive jurisdiction of European data protection law. GDPR applies to the processing of personal data in the context of activities of a controller or processor (see the discussion of these terms and GDPR in the Data Protection section below) in the EU, regardless of where the processing takes place. GDPR asserts prescriptive jurisdiction over personal data processing activities anywhere in the world related to offering goods or services to, or monitoring the behaviour of, Europeans.

Police officers can arrest a person within their state's territory. An extradition order is required in order to arrest a criminal outside of the state. Extradition is governed by bilateral treaties and is only allowed if the crime is considered a crime in both states. The Budapest Convention, which mandates the inclusion of computer crimes in extradition procedures, serves as a legal basis for extradition between states without a bilateral treaty. Extradition requests for cybercrime suspects can sometimes be denied because there is no extradition treaty, the act was not criminal in both countries, or when there are concerns over treatment the accused will face.

States can order residents within their jurisdiction to produce data under their control, even if the data is stored outside the state's territory. States can also request mutual legal assistance from other states, but the process is often slow. Alternatives to this process include gathering evidence directly under the Budapest Convention which imposes requirements on states to provide mutual legal assistance and preserve electronic evidence in the investigation of cybercrime.

Technological intervention, such as content filtering, can be used by states or individuals to enforce laws or reduce the risk of legal consequences. States can enforce filtering by ordering it directly or by issuing orders to in-state internet service providers (ISPs) to block the receipt of offending content. Out-of-state entities that host offending content can also initiate filtering to limit transfers to states where it may result in liability.

Data sovereignty refers to a state's right to regulate and enforce jurisdiction over data stored within its territory. With the growth of cloud computing, the physical location of data storage has become less relevant, which has raised concerns about the number of states that might seek to enforce their jurisdiction over such data. Some states have responded to these concerns by mandating local storage and processing (localization) for certain types of data. The EU, for instance, has a localization requirement for personal data.

In rem jurisdiction (power over property) allows a state to assert control over property within its territory, and this power has been applied to seize and forfeit servers and domain names involved in illegal activities.

Privacy

Privacy law is about the legal right of a person to be free from intrusion by others into their personal affairs, also known as the "right to be left alone." In the context of cybersecurity, privacy law often arises in the context of electronic surveillance and related investigatory activity. This area of law is constantly evolving in response to new technologies and use cases, including those enabled by cloud data processing services.

The right to privacy is widely recognized as a human right, including for the reasons and examples set out the Democratic Values section of the Privacy chapter of this book. However, the right is not absolute and is subject to limitations and exceptions. The application of privacy principles to data, such as electronic communications, has evolved over time and is currently internationally accepted. The interpretation and implementation of privacy rights, however, varies among countries. Expectations of privacy can also vary between different societies and according to the nature of a person's relationship with the intruding party. As people rely on third-party cloud services for more personal aspects of their lives, privacy concerns over the data processed through these systems will lead to new legislation.

Metadata, the data that describe other data, is often treated differently from content data in privacy laws. Private information is disclosed through metadata such as URLs (website addresses), and location data from personal mobile data communications.

68

There is no harmonization of legal standards and procedures for lawful interception of online data. Service providers, such as communication companies, are usually subject to local laws that require them to provide facilities and technical assistance for lawful interception. As encryption becomes more widespread, states are facing difficulties accessing plaintext or unencrypted messages.

Providers of public communication services are usually restricted from intercepting communications that pass through their networks. Efforts to intercept communications on a third-party network is considered a crime under computer intrusion laws. Interception by a person on their own non-public network, such as on their LAN, may or may not be subject to computer crime legislation. In-house interception activities may be limited by privacy and data protection laws. Some privacy violations, such as unauthorized interceptions of communications or intrusion into data, can be prosecuted by the state as crimes.

"I lost my wallet and my identity was stolen.

On the bright side, I got it back in the mail... with a note.

The note said, 'It sucks to be you.'"

Data Protection

There are laws that govern how personal data is collected, processed, and stored. The laws are based on privacy principles, but they also address issues relevant to modern data processing techniques. The focus is on protecting individual rights to personal data. Data protection laws provide remedies for individuals whose privacy rights have been violated, such as the ability to seek monetary compensation through a legal action. Some violations of privacy, such as unauthorized interception of communications, are defined as crimes.

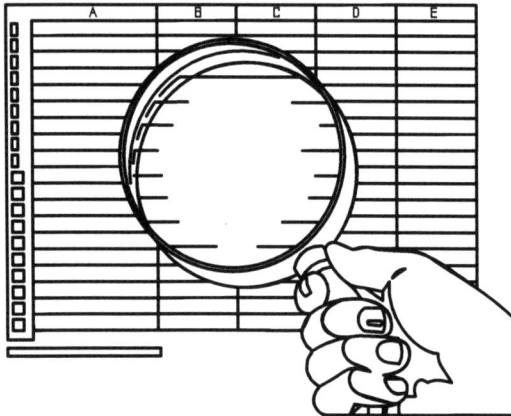

EU General Data Protection Regulation

The EU data protection law, referred to as GDPR, is meant to protect the privacy rights of individuals who are potentially identifiable through their communications. GDPR requires organizations to consider data protection from inception, and to implement measures that minimize the risk of data breaches. Implementation includes both technical and organizational measures that are appropriate for the risk level involved in the processing activity.

The definition of "personal data" under EU data protection law is broad and includes any information related to an identified or identifiable natural person. The definition covers not only obvious personal identifiers but also other factors that can lead to the identification of an individual. The term "personally identifiable information" or PII is often used in the US and may have different interpretations in different contexts, but it is not the same as "personal data".

EU data protection law has global impact through contract requirements imposed on non-EU data processors. It covers the processing of data – i.e. collection, recording, organization and storage. It also covers control of data, which means determining the purposes of the data and the methods by which it is processed.

There are principles for the lawful processing of personal data. They are: lawfulness, fairness, transparency, purpose limitation, data minimization, accuracy, storage limitation, integrity and confidentiality. Practitioners must be aware of sensitive personal data (e.g., racial origin, political opinions, and health data) which triggers additional protections and regulatory scrutiny. Consent for processing personal data is sometimes required and must be informed, clear, specific, and given freely.

The definitions of "processing" and "controller" and "processor" under GDPR make clear the roles and responsibilities of the two entities with respect to data. Processing is defined as any action taken with respect to personal data, including collection, recording, organization, and storage. The controller is the entity that determines the purposes and means of processing personal data, while the processor is the entity that carries out the processing on behalf of the controller.

Under law, controllers and processors must implement appropriate technical and organizational measures to ensure an appropriate level of security for processing personal data. Compliance requires appropriate technical measures as well as administrative management and oversight. GDPR provides examples of appropriate security measures, which include encryption. Security certifications help but are not considered guarantees of compliance with the law.

The transfer of personal data outside of the European Economic Area (EEA) is generally prohibited under GDPR. However, transfers can be made if the receiving country or international governmental organization has been found by the European Commission to have adequate legal protections in place. The process of obtaining an adequacy decision is initiated by the receiving state and often takes years of technical evaluation and diplomatic negotiation.

Data Breach Notification

The EU was first to impose requirements mandating the notification of personal data breaches to data subjects (individuals). The US has also started imposing a general duty to notify affected persons of personal data breaches. A personal data breach is defined as an accidental or unlawful destruction, loss, alteration, unauthorized disclosure of, or access to, personal data. The processor must first promptly notify the controller of the breach, and the controller must then notify the relevant supervisory authority, all within 72 hours. If the breach is likely to result in a high risk to the rights and freedoms of individuals, the controller must communicate the circumstances of the breach to these individuals. Communication to data subjects might, in some jurisdictions, be avoided if the controller has implemented measures to limit the harm caused by the breach, such as encryption because encryption reduces the potential harm that may come to data subjects.

GDPR carries significant legal risks for companies. This includes criminal prosecution, legal claims, enforcement notices, and large administrative fines. GDPR grants authority to impose fines of up to 4% of a company's annual worldwide turnover. Companies must assess and manage this risk at senior leadership levels and comply with all GDPR requirements.

Crimes Against Information Systems

Cybercrime generally refers to three categories of criminal activity: financial fraud using cyberspace, distribution of criminal content and hate speech over the internet, and crimes against cyberspace infrastructure such as computer system intrusion.

Early computer crime laws mainly focused on unauthorized intrusion into computer systems or improper modification of their contents. However, these laws became inadequate when DoS and DDoS (Denial of Service, e.g. overwhelming a computer system's processing power) attacks emerged. Currently, computer crime laws prohibit acts that cause a degradation in the performance of an information system, which includes Denial of Service.

Many legal systems prohibit the act of intercepting electronic communications without authorization, which is considered a violation of privacy. The penalties for this type of crime are often more severe if the communication is intercepted during its transmission on public networks. The production or distribution of tools with the intention of facilitating illegal activities against information systems is also considered a crime in many countries.

The penalties for committing a crime against information systems vary across countries and jurisdictions. Some people argue for longer sentences in cases where the acts cause significant damage to human welfare or national security.

Hacking Back

The absence of a specific legal basis for "hacking back" (retaliation by a company against their presumed cyberattacker) has made the practice controversial. Many warn against "hacking back" due to the potential for significant harm (including retaliating against the wrong party and/or inducing more attacks) and the risk of prosecution. The deployment of any such countermeasures is likely to cause friction where different states are involved and may also pose risks to innocent third parties. As a result, the majority of states have rejected any notion of "self-help" in the context of cybersecurity, and instead maintain a preference for the use of state-led responses to cyberattacks, such as diplomatic and legal measures.

Contract Law

A "contract" is a legally binding agreement between two or more parties. To be considered a contract, the agreement must show evidence of enforceability, such as consideration (value provided to each party) and intention to create a legal relationship. The specific time at which a contract is formed in online transactions can vary based on different legal systems but usually occurs once an offer has been transmitted and accepted.

Warranties are promises in contracts regarding the quality or legal status of goods or services, or the adequacy of information provided by one party. State contract laws usually add implied minimum warranties concerning the quality of goods and services. These include objective quality of goods, subjective quality of goods, and objective quality of services. Objective quality of goods refers to the promise that the goods delivered will be satisfactory to a normal buyer, while subjective quality of goods refers to the promise that the goods will meet the specific purpose of the buyer, who must disclose this purpose in advance. Objective quality of services refers to the promise that the service provider will exercise due care in delivering the service.

In the context of information and communications technology, it is common for vendors to attempt to exclude implied warranties, but it is more difficult to exclude in contracts with consumers. Limitations and exclusions of liability restrict financial responsibility for losses that may arise from the contracting relationship.

An exclusion of liability seeks to avoid financial responsibility for certain types of financial loss, while a limitation of liability limits financial liability to a fixed sum or formula. These exclusions and limitations are often seen as a risk-reduction tool. However, they are viewed with suspicion by most contract law systems, especially when contracting with consumers.

In the event of a breach of contract, the non-breaching party has various remedies available, such as damages, recission, specific performance, and contractually mandated remedies. The severity of the breach often determines the type of remedy available. Damages are the most common remedy and aim to restore the financial expectation of the non-breaching party (i.e. putting the non-breaching party in the position they would have been without a breach). Recission is a more extreme remedy, used when the breach is severe, which declares the contract at an end and excuses the non-breaching party from further performance. Specific performance is also an extreme remedy and is reserved for situations where the breaching party is able take a simple action that satisfies the non-breaching party. Contractually mandated remedies, specified in the contract, can also be available but are often treated with suspicion by courts. Remedies are cumulative, meaning that a party can request multiple remedies for a single breach of contract.

Negligence

Negligence law (a part of "Tort" law) imposes a duty of care on a person to take reasonable steps to avoid causing harm to others. Negligence is a common basis of liability in many contexts, including cybersecurity, as individuals and organizations have a duty to take reasonable steps to protect against foreseeable harm. This duty includes taking steps to keep personal information secure and to prevent unauthorized access to confidential information. The victim must prove that the other party's conduct caused them harm. This obligation means that the victim must demonstrate that the harm would not have occurred but for the other party's conduct.

Product Liability

Product liability law is also relevant to cybersecurity. It imposes liability on manufacturers and sellers for harm caused by products that are not reasonably safe. This liability can arise from defects in the design, manufacturing, or labeling of the product, or from a failure to provide adequate warnings or instructions. In the context of cybersecurity, this can include liability for harm caused by defective software or hardware products, or for harm caused by a failure to provide adequate security measures.

Vicarious Liability

Vicarious liability is a legal concept where an employer can be held responsible for the wrongful acts of their employees if those acts were committed within the scope of the employment relationship. Employers can avoid vicarious liability by insisting that employees act in lawful ways. This can be achieved through the development and enforcement of policies such as acceptable use policies, staff security standards, and employment policies.

Joint and Several Liability

Joint and several liability means that more than one party can be held responsible for causing harm to a single victim, and *any* of the responsible parties can be held liable for the *full* amount of damages awarded to the victim. This principle can become an issue when one of the defendants has limited financial resources or is located in a foreign jurisdiction where it is difficult to enforce a judgment. Companies should be mindful of this principle when working with partners or collaborators who may not have the financial resources to cover their share of a damages award in the event of a data protection violation.

Conclusion

The laws and regulations of each jurisdiction where a business operates will significantly affect business operations. The need to understand and comply with local data protection, privacy, and security laws is important for businesses operating online. All businesses need to be aware of the extra-territorial reach of certain laws and regulations.

Cybersecurity and digital identity practitioners need to be aware of the risks not only to their employer, but, should they ever be tempted or instructed to break criminal law, also to their own personal reputation, safety and liberty. Practitioners may personally face consequences for their actions, regardless of whatever incentives may have been provided them by their employer.

Seeking the advice of experienced legal counsel will help to mitigate legal risk. This chapter provides information about legal principles and examples of laws and regulations. It is not legal advice. For legal advice, please consult a lawyer.

Conclusion

"I have the only identity where if it was stolen...

The person who bought it would ask for a refund."

In order to develop policies that protect the digital identities of online service users, organizations must weigh potential threats to cybersecurity, threats to user privacy, human factors, and laws and regulations. Organizations need to weigh these issues when considering protecting the organization's assets and future prospects as well as the privacy and digital identity of their users.

Risk assessment for digital identity involves: identification and estimation of degree of hazard, assessment of the company's exposure and vulnerability, and estimation of risk in terms of likelihood of threat occurrence and severity of outcome. Risk managers need to conduct risk assessments, and based on the information they obtain, make decisions about which risks are acceptable, tolerable, or intolerable.

Cybersecurity risks include unauthorized access, availability issues, impersonation, and other types of fraudulent claims. Organizations should consider potential impacts to the confidentiality, integrity, and availability of information, and information systems.

Human factors are vital. Secure communication systems need to be user-friendly and not impose excessive cognitive burden on users. Research has shown that policies designed by security experts are often bypassed by employees because they demand too much effort and time and are, thus, ineffective. Digital identity management processes should be simple to use and designed such that mistakes are easy to fix. The idea is to fit the task to the human rather than the other way around.

Privacy-preserving technologies increase trust and minimize risk. Services should collect only essential data, minimize the replication and retention of data, cut down on linkages among the collected data, and avoid centralization of data. Data confidentiality can be achieved using cryptography. Privacy technology limits the information that is able to be leaked to potential adversaries, and ensuring, to the extent possible, that any data that are leaked cannot be linked to specific individuals.

Legal risk management involves understanding the laws and regulations that apply in all the jurisdictions in which an organization operates. The organization must consider the large number of laws and regulations, varying laws and enforcement authority across multiple jurisdictions, as well as the complexities of private law and regulatory systems.

Juggling jurisdictional civil and criminal laws, risk assessment, human factors, online privacy, and threats from unknown adversaries is very challenging and costly to all organizations.

This book has introduced the challenges of protection of digital identity and information systems and also the methods by which these challenges can be met.

"By encrypting all our data, the hackers can't read it, our unauthorized personnel can't read it, and, I'm afraid, neither can we."

Digital Identity and Cybersecurity Dictionary

A

2FA: Two factor authentication, a form of multi-factor authentication.

AAL: Authentication assurance level.

Access: To make contact with one or more functions of an online, digital service.

Access control mechanism: Security measures designed to detect and deny unauthorized access and permit authorized access to an information system or a physical facility.

Access control: The process of granting or denying specific requests for or attempts to: obtain and use information and related information processing services; and enter specific physical facilities.

Access: The ability and means to communicate with or otherwise interact with a system, to use system resources to handle information, to gain knowledge of the information the system contains, or to control system components and functions.

Accidental insider: An employee who accidentally introduces cybersecurity risk due to poor cybersecurity practices, such as accidentally click on a suspicious phishing link.

Actions: Using command and control of the installed ransomware to copy, destroy, or alter data, either immediately or in the future.

Active attack: An actual assault perpetrated by an intentional threat source that attempts to alter a system, its resources, its data, or its operations.

Active content: Software that is able to automatically carry out or trigger actions without the explicit intervention of a user.

Activation: The process of inputting an activation factor into a multi-factor authenticator to enable its use for authentication.

Active attack: An attack on the authentication protocol where the attacker transmits data to the Claimant, Credential Service Provider (CSP), verifier, or Relying Party (RP). Examples of active attacks include man-in-the-middle, impersonation, and session hijacking.

Administrative privileges: Permissions that allow a computer user to perform certain functions on a system, such as installing software and changing configuration settings.

Administrator: A person who administers a computer system or network and has access to the administrator account which has wide, sometimes complete, access to all data on the system, i.e. an "all-access" pass.

Advanced persistent threat: A long-term stealth cyberattack. Also a group, such as a state actor, with advanced cyberattack capabilities.

Advanced persistent threat: An adversary that possesses sophisticated levels of expertise and significant resources which allow it to create opportunities to achieve its objectives by using multiple attack vectors (e.g., cyber, physical, and deception).

Adversary: An individual, group, organization, or government that conducts or has the intent to conduct detrimental activities.

Air gap: To physically separate or isolate a system from other systems or networks.

Alert: A notification that a specific attack has been detected or directed at an organization's information systems.

All source intelligence: Analyzing threat information from multiple sources, disciplines, and agencies. Synthesizing and placing intelligence information in context; drawing insights about the possible implications.

Allowlist: A list of entities that are considered trustworthy and are granted access or privileges.

Analyze: Highly specialized reviewing and evaluation of incoming cybersecurity information to determine its usefulness for intelligence.

Antispyware software: A program that specializes in detecting and blocking or removing forms of spyware.

Antivirus software: A program that monitors a computer or network to detect or identify major types of malicious code and to prevent or contain malware incidents. Sometimes by removing or neutralizing the malicious code.

Antivirus: Software used to prevent, detect, and remove malware.

Applicant: A Subject undergoing the processes of enrollment and identity proofing.

Application: Software installed on a system.

Approved cryptography: Federal Information Processing Standard (FIPS)-approved or NIST recommended. An algorithm or technique that is either 1) specified in a FIPS or NIST Recommendation, or 2) adopted in a FIPS or NIST Recommendation.

APT: Advanced persistent threat.

Assertion: A statement from a verifier to an RP that contains information about a Subscriber.

Assertion reference: A data object, created in conjunction with an assertion, that identifies the verifier and includes a pointer to the full assertion held by the verifier.

Asset: A person, structure, facility, information, and records, information technology systems and resources, material, process, relationships, or reputation that has value.

Asymmetric cryptography: Public key cryptography.

Asymmetric keys: Two related keys, comprised of a public key and a private key, that are used to perform complementary operations such as encryption and decryption or signature verification and generation.

Attack method: The manner or technique and means an adversary may use in an assault on information or an information system.

Attack mode: Attack method.

Attack path: The steps that an adversary takes or may take to plan, prepare for, and execute an attack.

Attack pattern: Similar cyber events or behaviors that may indicate an attack has occurred or is occurring, resulting in a security violation or a potential security violation.

Attack signature: A characteristic or distinctive pattern that can be searched for or that can be used in matching to previously identified attacks.

Attack surface: The set of ways in which an adversary can enter a system and potentially cause damage. An information system's characteristics that permit an adversary to probe, attack, or maintain presence in the information system.

Attack vector: Attack method.

Attack: An attempt to gain unauthorized access to system services, resources, or information, or an attempt to compromise system integrity.

Attacker: An individual, group, organization, or government that executes an attack. A party acting with malicious intent to compromise an information system.

Attacker-in-the-middle attack: Man-in-the-middle attack.

Attribute: A quality or characteristic ascribed to someone or something.

Attribute value: A complete statement asserting a property of a Subscriber, independent of format. For example, for the attribute birthday, a value could be 12/1/1980 or December 1, 1980.

Authentication: The process of verifying the identity or other attributes of an entity (user, process, or device). The process of verifying the source and integrity of data.

Authentication factor: The three types of authentication factors are something you know, something you have, and something you are. Every authenticator has one or more authentication factors.

Authentication intent: The process of confirming the Claimant's intent to authenticate or reauthenticate by including a process requiring user intervention in the authentication flow. Some authenticators (e.g., OTP devices) establish authentication intent as part of their operation, others require a specific step, such as pressing a button, to establish intent. Authentication intent is a countermeasure against use by malware of the endpoint as a proxy for authenticating an attacker without the Subscriber's knowledge.

Authentication protocol: A defined sequence of messages between a Claimant and a Verifier that demonstrates that the Claimant has possession and control of one or more valid authenticators to establish their identity, and, optionally, demonstrates that the Claimant is communicating with the intended Verifier.

Authentication secret: A generic term for any secret value that an attacker could use to impersonate the Subscriber in an authentication protocol. These are further divided into short-term authentication secrets, which are only useful to an attacker for a limited period of time, and long-term authentication secrets, which allow an attacker to impersonate the Subscriber until they are manually reset. The authenticator secret is the canonical example of a long-term authentication secret, while the authenticator output, if it is different from the authenticator secret, is usually a short-term authentication secret.

Authenticator: Token. Something the Claimant possesses and controls (typically a cryptographic module or password) that is used to authenticate the Claimant's identity.

Authentication assurance level: A category describing the strength of the authentication process.

Authenticator output: The output value generated by an authenticator. The ability to generate valid authenticator outputs on demand proves that the Claimant possesses and controls the authenticator. Protocol messages sent to the Verifier are dependent upon the authenticator output, but they may or may not explicitly contain it.

Authenticator secret: The secret value contained within an authenticator.

Authenticator type: A category of authenticators with common characteristics. Some authenticator types provide one authentication factor, others provide two.

Authenticity: A property achieved through cryptographic methods of being genuine and being able to be verified and trusted, resulting in confidence in the validity of a transmission, information or a message, or sender of information or a message.

Authoritative source: An entity that has access to, or verified copies of, accurate information from an issuing source such that a CSP can confirm the validity of the identity evidence supplied by an Applicant during identity proofing. An issuing source may also be an authoritative source. Often, authoritative sources are determined by a policy decision of the agency or CSP before they can be used in the identity proofing validation phase.

Authorization: A process of determining, by evaluating applicable access control information, whether a Subject is allowed to have the specified types of access to a particular resource. The process or act of granting access privileges or the access privileges as granted.

AV: Antivirus.

Availability: Ensuring timely and reliable access to and use of information and preventing disruption in information access.

B

Backdoor: An undocumented, private, or less-detectible method of gaining remote access to a computer, bypassing authentication measures.

Backup: A copy of files, data and software made to facilitate recovery of a system.

Bearer assertion: The assertion a party presents as proof of identity, where possession of the assertion itself is sufficient proof of identity for the assertion bearer.

Binding: An association between a Subscriber identity and an authenticator or given Subscriber session.

Biometric reference: One or more stored biometric samples, templates, or models attributed to an individual and used as the object of biometric comparison. For example, a facial image stored digitally on a passport, fingerprint minutiae template on a National ID card or Gaussian Mixture Model for speaker recognition in a database.

Biometric sample: An analog or digital representation of biometric characteristics prior to biometric feature extraction. An example is a record containing a fingerprint image.

Biometrics: Automated recognition of individuals based on their biological and behavioral characteristics.

BIA: Business impact analysis.

Black hat: Criminals who seek to access systems to exploit vulnerabilities for cybercrime.

Blocklist: A list of entities that are blocked or denied privileges or access.

Blue Team: A group that defends an organization's information systems when mock attackers (i.e., the Red Team) attack, typically as part of an operational exercise conducted according to rules established and monitored by a neutral group (i.e., the White Team). Also, a group that conducts operational vulnerability evaluations and recommends mitigation techniques to customers who need an independent technical review of their cybersecurity posture.

Bot master: The controller of a botnet that, from a remote location, provides direction to the compromised computers in the botnet.

Bot: A computer connected to the Internet that has been surreptitiously or secretly compromised with malicious logic to perform activities under remote the command and control of a remote administrator. A member of a larger collection of compromised computers known as a botnet.

Botnet: A network of hijacked computers and devices infected with malware and remotely controlled by a criminal.

Brute force attack: Automatic entry of millions of combinations of characters in repetitive login attempts until the criminal successfully obtains a password.

Bug fix patch: Repairs functionality issues in software.

Bug: An unexpected and relatively small defect, fault, flaw, or imperfection in an information system or device.

Build security in: A set of principles, practices, and tools to design, develop, and evolve information systems and software that enhance resistance to vulnerabilities, flaws, and attacks.

Business continuity planning: Disaster recovery planning.

Business impact analysis: Predicts how disruptions or incidents will harm an organization's operations, business processes, systems, and finances.

C

Capability: The means to accomplish a mission, function, or objective.

CAPTCHA: Completely Automated Public Turing test to tell Computers and Humans Apart. An interactive feature added to web forms to distinguish whether a human or automated agent is using the form. Typically, it requires entering text corresponding to a distorted image or a sound stream.

Challenge-response protocol: An authentication protocol where the Verifier sends the Claimant a challenge (usually a random value or nonce) that the Claimant combines with a secret (such as by hashing the challenge and a shared secret together, or by applying a private key operation to the challenge) to generate a response that is sent to the Verifier. The Verifier can independently verify the response generated by the Claimant (such as by re-computing the hash of the challenge and the shared secret and comparing to the response, or performing a public key operation on the response) and establish that the Claimant possesses and controls the secret.

Chief Information Officer/Chief Information Security Officer: Person responsible for ensuring the security of systems and data in an organization.

CIO/CISO: Chief Information Officer/Chief Information Security Officer.

Cipher: Cryptographic algorithm.

Ciphertext: Data or information in its encrypted form.

CIRT: Cyber incident response team.

Claimant: A Subject whose identity is to be verified using one or more authentication protocols.

Claimed identity: An Applicant's declaration of unvalidated and unverified personal attributes.

Cloud computing: The use of remote servers hosted on the internet. Cloud computing allows users to access a shared pool of computing resources, including networks, servers, applications, or services, on demand and from anywhere.

Cloud service provider: A company that provides cloud computing services, e.g. Amazon AWS.

Collect and operate: Specialized denial and deception operations and collection of cybersecurity information that may be used to develop intelligence.

Collection operations: Executing collection using appropriate strategies and within the priorities established through the collection management process.

Command and control: A computer on the internet used by the criminal to send commands to systems compromised by ransomware and to receive stolen data.

Computer forensics: Digital forensics.

Computer network defense analysis: Using defensive measures and information collected from a variety of sources to identify, analyze, and report events that occur or might occur within the network in order to protect information, information systems, and networks from threats.

Computer network defense infrastructure support: Testing, implementing, deploying, maintaining, reviewing, and administering the infrastructure hardware and software that are required to effectively manage the computer network defense service provider network and resources; monitors network to actively remediate unauthorized activities.

Computer network defense: The actions taken to defend against unauthorized activity within computer networks.

Computer security incident: Event or incident.

Confidentiality: The prevention of damage to, protection of, and restoration of computers, electronic communications systems, electronic communications services, wire communication, and electronic communication, including information, to ensure its availability, integrity, authentication, confidentiality, and nonrepudiation.

Consequence: The effect of an event, incident, or occurrence. The effect of a loss of confidentiality, integrity or availability of information or an information system on an organization's operations, its assets, on individuals, other organizations, or on national interests.

Contingency planning: Disaster recovery planning.

Continuity of operations plan: A document that sets forth procedures for the continued performance of core capabilities and critical operations during any disruption or potential disruption.

Core attributes: The set of identity attributes the CSP has determined and documented to be required for identity proofing.

Credential: An object or data structure that authoritatively binds an identity – via an identifier or identifiers – and (optionally) additional attributes, to at least one authenticator possessed and controlled by a Subscriber. A credential is issued, stored, and maintained by the CSP. Copies of information from the credential can be possessed by the Subscriber, typically in the form of a one or more digital certificates that are often contained, along with their associated private keys, in an authenticator.

Credential service provider: A trusted entity whose functions include identity proofing Applicants to the identity service and the registration of authenticators to subscriber accounts. A CSP may be an independent third party.

Criminal: Threat agent.

Critical infrastructure and key resources: Critical infrastructure.

Critical infrastructure: Physical and virtual assets that are essential to the operation of an organization or a state.

Cross-site request forgery: An attack in which a Subscriber currently authenticated to an RP and connected through a secure session browses to an attacker's website, causing the Subscriber to unknowingly invoke unwanted actions at the RP. For example, if a bank website is vulnerable to a CSRF attack, it may be possible for a Subscriber to unintentionally authorize a large money transfer, merely by viewing a malicious link in a webmail message while a connection to the bank is open in another browser window.

Cross-site scripting: A vulnerability that allows attackers to inject malicious code into an otherwise benign website. These scripts acquire the permissions of scripts generated by the target website and can therefore compromise the confidentiality and integrity of data transfers between the website and client. Websites are vulnerable if they display user-supplied data from requests or forms without sanitizing the data so that it is not executable.

Cryptanalysis: The operations performed in defeating or circumventing cryptographic protection of information by applying mathematical techniques and without an initial knowledge of the key employed in providing the protection. The study of mathematical techniques for attempting to defeat or circumvent cryptographic techniques and/or information systems security.

Cryptocurrency: Tradable electronic tokens such as bitcoin.

Cryptographic algorithm: A well-defined computational procedure that takes variable inputs, including a cryptographic key, and produces an output.

Cryptographic authenticator: An authenticator that proves possession of an authentication secret through direct communication, via the endpoint, with a Verifier.

Cryptographic key: A value used to control cryptographic operations, such as decryption, encryption, signature generation, or signature verification.

Cryptographic module: A set of hardware, software, and/or firmware that implements approved security functions (including cryptographic algorithms and key generation).

Cryptography: The use of mathematical techniques to provide security services, such as confidentiality, data integrity, entity authentication, and data origin authentication. The art or science concerning the principles, means, and methods for converting plaintext into ciphertext and for restoring encrypted ciphertext to plaintext.

Cryptology: The mathematical science that deals with cryptanalysis and cryptography.

CSP: Cloud service provider (in computing) or Credential service provider (in digital identity).

CSRF: Cross-site request forgery.

Customer service and technical support: Addressing problems, installing, configuring, troubleshooting, and providing maintenance and training in response to customer requirements or inquiries (e.g., tiered-level customer support).

Cyber ecosystem: The interconnected information infrastructure of interactions among persons, processes, data, and information and communications technologies, along with the environment and conditions that influence those interactions.

Cyber exercise: A planned event during which an organization simulates a cyber disruption to develop or test capabilities such as preventing, detecting, mitigating, responding to or recovering from the disruption.

Cyber incident response plan: Incident response plan.

Cyber incident response team: An internal team for incident response.

Cyber incident: Event or incident.

Cyber infrastructure: An electronic information and communications systems and services and the information contained therein. The information and communications systems and services composed of all hardware and software that process, store, and communicate information, or any combination of all of these elements: Processing includes the creation, access, modification, and destruction of information. Storage includes paper, magnetic, electronic, and all other media types. Communications include sharing and distribution of information.

Cyber kill chain: A series of steps that trace the stages of a cyberattack from the criminal's early reconnaissance stages to the criminal's exfiltration of data. Reconnaissance: the observation stage; criminals assess from the outside to identify targets and tactics. Intrusion: access into the systems, often leveraging malware or security vulnerabilities. Exploitation: taking advantage of vulnerabilities, and delivering malicious code. Privilege escalation: criminals often need more privileges to get access to more data. Therefore, once inside a system, they use techniques to increase their own access privileges, often to the most powerful "administrator" status.

Cyber operations planning: Performing in-depth joint targeting and cyber planning process. Gathering information and develops detailed Operational Plans and Orders supporting requirements. Conducting strategic and operational-level planning across the full range of operations for integrated information and cyberspace operations.

Cyber operations: Performing activities to gather evidence on criminal or foreign intelligence entities in order to mitigate possible or real-time threats, protecting against espionage or insider threats, foreign sabotage, international terrorist activities, or supporting other intelligence activities.

Cyberattack: Information security event caused by a threat agent.

Cyberattacker: Threat agent.

Cybercrime: Technology-enabled crimes, generally for personal or financial gain.

Cybercriminal: Threat agent.

Cyberespionage: The practice of theft of confidential information for the purposes of covert, unethical and/or illegal competition among individuals, organizations or nations.

Cybersecurity: People, processes, and technologies which prevent damage to, protect, and restore computers, electronic communications systems and services, and information to ensure information confidentiality, integrity, and availability.

D

Data administration: Developing and administering databases and/or data management systems that allow for the storage, query, and utilization of data.

Data aggregation: The process of gathering and combining data from different sources, so that the combined data reveals new information. The new information is more

WHO AM I NOT?

sensitive than the individual data elements themselves and the person who aggregates the data was not granted access to the totality of the information.

Data breach: The unauthorized movement or disclosure of sensitive information to a party, usually outside the organization, that is not authorized to have or see the information.

Data integrity: The property that data is complete, intact, and trusted and has not been modified or destroyed in an unauthorized or accidental manner.

Data leakage: Data breach.

Data loss prevention: A set of procedures and mechanisms to stop sensitive data from leaving a security boundary.

Data loss: The result of unintentionally or accidentally deleting data, forgetting where it is stored, or exposure to an unauthorized party.

Data mining: The process or techniques used to analyze large sets of existing information to discover previously unrevealed patterns or correlations.

Data spill: Data breach.

Data theft: The deliberate or intentional act of stealing of information.

Data: A representation of facts, concepts, or instructions.

Database: An organized collection of data stored and accessed electronically.

Decipher: To convert enciphered text to plain text by means of a cryptographic system.

Decode: To convert encoded text to plain text by means of a code.

Decrypt: A generic term encompassing decode and decipher.

Decryption: The process of transforming ciphertext into its original plaintext. The process of converting encrypted data back into its original form.

Defence-in-depth: A cybersecurity concept in which multiple layers of security are used to protect the integrity of information. These layers can include antivirus software, firewalls, hierarchical passwords, intrusion detection, and biometric identification.

Delivery: Distribution of the ransomware to the target system, e.g. by an email phishing attachment.

Denial of service: A cyberattack that successfully prevents or impairs the normal functioning of systems by using all of its capacity. Such an attack commonly uses thousands of devices accessing a website simultaneously and continually, leading to overload and inability to deliver webpages to legitimate users.

Derived attribute value: A statement asserting a property of a Subscriber without necessarily containing identity information, independent of format. For example, instead of requesting the attribute birthday, a derived value could be older than 18. Instead of requesting the attribute for physical address, a derived value could be currently residing in this district.

Designed-in security: Build security in.

Detect: Develop and implement the appropriate activities to identify the occurrence of a cyberattack.

Devices: System equipment, including computers, servers, printers and telephones.

Differential backup: Incremental backup.

Digital authentication: The process of establishing confidence in user identities presented digitally to a system.

Digital forensics: The processes and specialized techniques for gathering, retaining, and analyzing system-related data, i.e. digital evidence, for investigative purposes. Collecting, processing, preserving, analyzing, and presenting computer-related evidence in support of network vulnerability, mitigation, and/or criminal, fraud, counterintelligence or law enforcement investigations.

Digital rights management: A form of access control technology to protect and manage use of digital content or devices in accordance with the content or device provider's intentions.

Digital signature: A value computed with a cryptographic process using a private key and then appended to a data object, thereby digitally signing the data. Digital signatures provide authenticity protection, integrity protection, and non-repudiation, but not confidentiality protection.

Disaster recovery planning: How to resume normal operations after a cyberattack.

Disruption: An event which causes unplanned interruption in operations or functions for an unacceptable length of time.

Distributed denial of service: A denial of service technique that uses numerous systems to perform the attack simultaneously. Denial of service.

DMARC: Domain-based message authentication, reporting and conformance.

DNS: Domain name system.

Domain name system: The "telephone book" for the internet used for both human-initiated actions such as visiting a website and machine-initiated actions such as running an update. It translates destinations such as "gmail.com" into a specific computer number such as "8.8.8.8" that a computer can understand.

Domain-based message authentication, reporting and conformance: Allows senders and receivers of email to improve and monitor protection of the domain name being used for fraudulent email.

DoS: Denial of service.

Double extortion schemes: Ransomware criminals steal sensitive data from the organization and encrypt the system files and demand ransom. However, with double extortion, even if the ransom is paid and the system files are decrypted, the criminals then threaten to publish or sell the stolen data unless the victim pays a second ransom.

Drive-by download: When a user unknowingly visits a malicious website where malware is surreptitiously automatically downloaded and installed.

Dynamic attack surface: The automated, on-the-fly changes of an information system's characteristics to thwart actions of an adversary.

E

Eavesdropping attack: An attack in which an attacker listens passively to the authentication protocol to capture information that can be used in a subsequent active attack to masquerade as the Claimant.

Education and training: Conducting training of personnel within pertinent subject domain; developing, planning, coordinating, delivering, and/or evaluating training courses, methods, and techniques as appropriate.

Electronic signature: Any mark in electronic form associated with an electronic document, applied with the intent to sign the document.

Encipher: To convert plaintext to ciphertext by means of a cryptographic system.

Encode: To convert plaintext to ciphertext by means of a code.

Encrypt: The generic term encompassing encipher and encode.

Encryption: A process of making electronically stored information unreadable to anyone not having the correct password or key. The process uses cryptography to convert plain (readable) text into cipher (unreadable) text to prevent anyone except the intended recipient from reading the data.

Encryption: The process of transforming plaintext into ciphertext. Converting data into a form that cannot be easily understood by unauthorized people.

Enrollment: The process through which an Applicant applies to become a Subscriber of a CSP and the CSP validates the Applicant's identity.

Enterprise risk management: A comprehensive approach to risk management that engages people, processes, and systems across an organization to improve the quality of decision making for managing risks that may hinder an organization's ability to achieve its objectives. Involves identifying mission dependencies on enterprise capabilities, identifying and prioritizing risks due to defined threats, implementing countermeasures to provide both a static risk posture and an effective dynamic response to active threats; and assessing enterprise performance against threats and adjusts countermeasures as necessary.

Entropy: A measure of the amount of uncertainty an attacker faces to determine the value of a secret. Entropy is usually stated in bits. A value having n bits of entropy has the same degree of uncertainty as a uniformly distributed n-bit random value.

Event: An observable occurrence in an information system or network. Sometimes provides an indication that an incident is occurring or at least raise the suspicion that an incident may be occurring.

Exfiltrate: Stealing and removing data from a compromised system. The unauthorized transfer of information from an information system.

Exploit: A technique to breach the security of a network or information system in violation of security policy.

Exploitation analysis: Analyzing collected information to identify vulnerabilities and potential for exploitation.

Exploitation: Taking advantage of cybersecurity vulnerabilities, and delivering malware into a system.

Exposure: The condition of being unprotected, thereby allowing access to information or access to capabilities that an attacker can use to enter a system or network.

F

Failure: The inability of a system or component to perform its required functions within specified performance requirements.

Feature patch: Adds new functions to the software.

Federation: A process that allows the conveyance of identity and authentication information across a set of networked systems.

Federation protocol and identity provider (IdP): An identity provider for a Federation process.

Firewall: A security barrier placed between two networks that controls the amount and type of network traffic that may pass between the two. The barrier protects local system resources from being accessed from the outside.

Forensics: Digital forensics.

H

Hacker: An unauthorized user, Black hat or White hat, who attempts to or gains access to an information system.

Hacktivist: Politically or ideologically motivated threat agent who aims to damage the organization.

Hash value: A numeric value resulting from applying a mathematical algorithm against a set of data such as a file.

Hashing: A process of applying a mathematical algorithm against a set of data to produce a numeric value (a "hash value") that represents the data. Mapping a bit string of arbitrary length to a fixed length bit string to produce the hash value.

Hazard: A natural or man-made source or cause of harm or difficulty.

I

IAL: Identity assurance Level.

ICT supply chain threat: A man-made threat achieved through exploitation of the information and communications technology (ICT) system's supply chain, including acquisition processes.

ICT: Information and communications technology.

Identify: Develop the organizational understanding to manage cybersecurity risk to systems, assets, data, and capabilities.

Identity and access management: The methods and processes used to manage Subjects and their authentication and authorizations to access specific objects.

Identity assurance level: A category that conveys the degree of confidence that the Applicant's claimed identity is their real identity.

Identity: Details describing who a person is on a system, e.g. their username. An attribute or set of attributes that uniquely describe a Subject within a given context.

Identity evidence: Information or documentation provided by the Applicant to support the claimed identity. Identity evidence may be physical (e.g. a driver license) or digital (e.g. an assertion generated and issued by a CSP based on the Applicant successfully authenticating to the CSP).

Identity proofing: The process by which a CSP collects, validates, and verifies information about a person.

Identity resolution: The process of collecting information about an Applicant in order to uniquely distinguish an individual within the context of the population the CSP serves.

IdP: Federation protocol and identity provider.

IDPS: Intrusion detection / prevention system.

IDS: Intrusion detection system.

Impact: The effect on organizational operations, organizational assets, individuals, other organizations, or national security interests of a loss of confidentiality, integrity, or availability of information or a system. Consequence.

Improper usage: A user violates the organization's acceptable computing-use policies.

Incident management: The management and coordination of activities associated with an actual or potential occurrence of an event that may result in adverse consequences to information or information systems.

Incident response plan: A set of predetermined and documented procedures to detect and respond to a cyber incident.

Incident response: Assess, document, and respond to incidents, restore an organization's systems, recover information, and reduce the risk of the cyberattack reoccurring.

Incident: An occurrence that actually or potentially results in adverse consequences to an information system or the information that the system processes, stores, or transmits and that may require a response action to mitigate the consequences. An occurrence that constitutes a violation or imminent threat of violation of security policies, security procedures, or acceptable use policies. Information security event.

Incremental backup: A backup that only records any changes made since the last backup.

Indicator: An occurrence or sign that an incident may have occurred or may be in progress.

Industrial control system: An information system used to control industrial processes such as manufacturing, product handling, production, and distribution or to control infrastructure assets.

Information and communications technology: Any information technology, equipment, or interconnected system or subsystem of equipment that processes, transmits, receives, or interchanges data or information.

Information assurance compliance: Overseeing, evaluating, and supporting the documentation, validation, and accreditation processes necessary to assure that new IT systems meet the organization's information assurance and security requirements; ensuring appropriate treatment of risk, compliance, and assurance from internal and external perspectives.

Information assurance: The measures that protect and defend information and information systems by ensuring their availability, integrity, and confidentiality.

Information security event: An event that affects the confidentiality, availability, or integrity of information.

Information security policy: An aggregate of directives, regulations, rules, and practices that prescribe how an organization manages, protects, and distributes information.

Information security: The protection of information and information systems from unauthorized access, use, disclosure, disruption, modification, or destruction in order to provide confidentiality, integrity, and availability.

Information sharing: An exchange of data, information, and/or knowledge to manage risks or respond to incidents.

Information system resilience: The ability of an information system to: continue to operate under adverse conditions or stress, even if in a degraded or debilitated state, while maintaining essential operational capabilities; and recover effectively in a timely manner.

Information system: An integrated set of components for collecting, storing, and processing data and for providing information, knowledge, and digital products, including the network and connected devices.

Information systems security operations: Overseeing the information assurance program of an information system in or outside the network environment.

Information technology: The use of computers, storage, networking and other physical devices, infrastructure and processes to create, process, store, secure and exchange all forms of electronic data.

Information: Organized or classified data.

Insider threat: Current or former employees, contractors, or other business partners who have or had authorized access to an organization's network, system, or data and intentionally misused that access to negatively affect the confidentiality, integrity, or availability of the organization's information or system.

Insider: Any person with authorized access to the organization's resources, including personnel, facilities, information, equipment, networks, or system.

Installation: Malware stored on a target organization's system.

Integrated risk management: The structured approach that enables an enterprise or organization to share risk information and risk analysis and to synchronize independent yet complementary risk management strategies to unify efforts across the organization.

Integrity: Guarding against improper information modification or destruction, and includes ensuring information non-repudiation and authenticity.

Intent: A state of mind or desire to achieve an objective.

Internet protocol: The method by which data is sent from one computer to another on the internet.

Interoperability: The ability of two or more systems or components to exchange information and to use the information that has been exchanged.

Intrusion detection / prevention system: Software that automates the process of monitoring the events occurring in a system and analyzing them for signs of possible incidents and attempting to stop detected possible incidents.

Intrusion detection system: Intrusion detection / prevention system.

Intrusion prevention system: Intrusion detection / prevention system.

Intrusion: An unauthorized act of bypassing the security mechanisms of a network or information system. Penetration.

Inventory: A listing of items including identification and location information.

Investigate: Investigation of cyber events and/or crimes of IT systems, networks, and digital evidence

Investigation: A systematic and formal inquiry into a qualified threat or incident using digital forensics and perhaps other traditional criminal inquiry techniques to determine the events that transpired and to collect evidence. Appling tactics, techniques, and procedures for a full range of investigative tools and processes to include but not limited to interview and interrogation techniques, surveillance, counter surveillance, and surveillance detection, and appropriately balancing the benefits of prosecution versus intelligence gathering.

IP: Either a) internet protocol or, b) intellectual property such as copyright or trade secrets.

IPS: Intrusion detection / prevention system.

Issuing source: An authority responsible for the generation of data, digital evidence (such as assertions), or physical documents that can be used as identity evidence.

IT asset: Asset.

IT: Information technology.

K

KBA: Knowledge-based authentication.

KBP: Knowledge-based proofing.

KBV: Knowledge-based verification.

Knowledge-based verification: Identity verification method based on knowledge of private information associated with the claimed identity.

Knowledge management: Managing and administering processes and tools that enable the organization to identify, document, and access intellectual capital and information content.

L

Lateral movement: Once in the system, criminals moving to other systems and accounts, in order to gain more control, including higher permissions, more data, or greater access.

Least privilege: The principle of giving a user only the rights to use the system that are required to perform the user's authorized tasks. This principle limits the damage that might result from the accidental, incorrect, or unauthorized use of a system.

Legal advice and advocacy: Legally sound advice and recommendations to leadership and staff on a variety of relevant topics within the pertinent subject domain; advocating legal and policy changes and making a case on behalf of client through a wide range of written and oral work products, including legal briefs and proceedings.

Likelihood: A weighted factor based on a subjective analysis of the probability that a given threat is capable of exploiting a vulnerability.

Log: A data file that records events that occur in a system as they occur, i.e. a record of what happens.

M

MAC: Message authentication code.

Machine learning and evolution: A field concerned with designing and developing artificial intelligence algorithms for automated knowledge discovery and innovation by information systems.

Macro virus: A type of malicious code that attaches itself to documents and uses the macro programming capabilities of the document's application to execute, replicate, and spread or propagate itself.

Malicious actors: Threat agents.

Malicious applet: A small application program that is automatically downloaded and executed and that performs an unauthorized function on an information system.

Malicious code: Program code intended to perform an unauthorized function or process that will have adverse impact on the confidentiality, integrity, or availability of an information system. Includes software, firmware, and scripts.

Malicious insider: Usually a disgruntled employee who steals or destroys the organization's information.

Malicious logic: Hardware, firmware, or software that is intentionally included or inserted in a system to perform an unauthorized function or process that will have adverse impact on the confidentiality, integrity, or availability of an information system.

Malware macros: A small program that can automate tasks in applications which attackers can use to gain access to and harm a system.

Malware: Malicious software designed to infiltrate or damage a system, or steal or harm use computing resources, without the owner's consent. Malware intended to perform an unauthorized process that will have adverse impact on the confidentiality, integrity, or availability of an information system. Forms include ransomware, virus, spyware (spying), adware (advertising), worm, and Trojan horse.

Man-in-the-middle attack: A cyberattack where the criminal secretly relays and possibly alters the communications between two parties who believe that they are directly communicating with each other, as the criminal has inserted herself between the two parties.

Managed service providers (MSPs): Outsourced contractors who assume the organization's responsibility to perform a range of processes and functions for the purpose of improved operations and reduced budgetary expenditures through the reduction of directly-employed staff.

Memorized secret: A password.

Message authentication code: A cryptographic checksum on data that uses a symmetric key to detect both accidental and intentional modifications of the data. MACs provide authenticity and integrity protection, but not non-repudiation protection.

MFA: Multi-factor authentication.

Mitigation: The application of one or more measures to reduce the likelihood of an unwanted occurrence and/or lessen its consequences. Implementing appropriate risk-reduction controls based on risk management priorities and analysis of alternatives.

Mobile code: Executable code that is normally transferred from its source to another computer system for execution. This transfer is often through the network (e.g., JavaScript embedded in a web page) but may transfer through physical media as well.

Moving target defense: The presentation of a dynamic attack surface, increasing an adversary's work factor necessary to probe, attack, or maintain presence in a cyber target.

MSP: Managed service providers.

Multi-factor authentication: Authentication is validated by using a combination of two or more different factors including: something you know (for example, a password), something you have (for example, a physical token), and/or something you are (for example, a fingerprint).

Multi-factor authenticator: An authenticator that provides more than one distinct authentication factor, such as a cryptographic authentication device with an integrated biometric sensor that is required to activate the device.

N

Network: An open communications medium, typically the Internet, used to transport messages between the Claimant and other parties. Unless otherwise stated, no assumptions are made about the network's security; it is assumed to be open and subject to active (e.g., impersonation, man-in-the-middle, session hijacking) and passive (e.g., eavesdropping) attack at any point between the parties (e.g., Claimant, Verifier, CSP, RP).

Network resilience: The ability of a network to: provide continuous operation (i.e., highly resistant to disruption and able to operate in a degraded mode if damaged); recover effectively if failure does occur; and scale to meet rapid or unpredictable demands.

Network security zone: A networking environment with a well-defined boundary and a standard of cybersecurity to network threats. Types of zones are distinguished by security requirements for interfaces, traffic control, data protection, host configuration control, and network configuration control.

Network services: Installing, configuring, testing, operating, maintaining, and managing networks and their firewalls, including hardware (e.g., hubs, bridges, switches, multiplexers, routers, cables, proxy servers, and protective distributor systems) and software that permit the sharing and transmission of all spectrum transmissions of information to support the security of information and information systems.

Non-repudiation: A property achieved through cryptographic methods to protect against an individual or entity falsely denying having performed a particular action related to data. Provides the capability to determine whether a given individual took a particular action such as creating information, sending a message, approving information, and receiving a message.

O

Obfuscation: Criminals trying to cover their tracks by laying false trails, compromising data, and clearing logs to confuse or slow down a forensics investigation.

Object: A passive information system-related entity containing or receiving information.

Offline: A network disconnected from the internet or a computer or server disconnected from any network, including the internet.

Online guessing attack: Brute force attack.

Operate and maintain: Providing the support, administration, and maintenance necessary to ensure effective and efficient IT system performance and security.

Operating system: The software master control application that runs a computer. It is the first computer program loaded when the computer is turned on, and its main component, the kernel, resides in memory at all times. The operating system sets the standards for all application programs (such as the Web server) that run in the computer. The applications communicate with the operating system for most user interface and file management operations.

Operational exercise: An action-based exercise where personnel rehearse reactions to an incident scenario, drawing on their understanding of plans and procedures, roles, and responsibilities. Also referred to as operations-based exercise.

Operational security: Protecting business plans and processes.

Operations technology: The hardware and software systems used to operate industrial control devices.

OS: Operating System.

Out-of-band: A separate method of communication not using the system. For example, a mobile phone call or Gmail email using a smartphone not connected to the system is "out-of-band".

Outsider threat: A person or group of persons external to an organization who are not authorized to access its assets and pose a potential risk to the organization and its assets.

Oversight and development: Providing leadership, management, direction, and/or development and advocacy so that all individuals and the organization may effectively conduct cybersecurity work.

P

PAD: Presentation attack detection.

Passive attack: An actual assault perpetrated by an intentional threat source that attempts to learn or make use of information from a system, but does not attempt to alter the system, its resources, its data, or its operations.

Passphrase: Instead of a password, a long phrase such as "FenceSoccerHappyBell". A passphrase is similar to a password in usage, but is generally longer for added security.

Password: A string of characters (letters, numbers and other symbols) that are used to authenticate an identity, to verify access authorization or to derive cryptographic keys. A type of authenticator comprised of a character string intended to be memorized or memorable by the Subscriber, permitting the Subscriber to demonstrate something they know as part of an authentication process.

Pen testing: Penetration testing.

Penetration testing: A method to gain assurance of the security of a system. A cybersecurity professional attempts to breach some or all of the system's security, using the same tools and techniques that a criminal might use.

Penetration: Intrusion.

Perimeter: The boundary between two network security zones through which traffic is routed.

Personal data: Personally identifiable information.

Personally identifiable information: Information which can be used to distinguish or trace an individual's identity, such as their name, social security number, biometric records, date and place of birth, mother's maiden name, passwords, credit card numbers, driver's license number, and bank account details, alone, or when combined with other personally identifiable information.

Phishing: An attack that uses text, email, or social media to fool users into clicking a malicious link or attachment. An attempt by a third party to solicit confidential information from an individual, group, or organization by mimicking or spoofing, a specific, usually well-known brand, usually for financial gain. Phishers attempt to trick users into disclosing personal data, such as credit card numbers, online banking credentials, and other sensitive information, which they may then use to commit fraudulent acts.

Personal identification number: A memorized secret typically consisting of only decimal digits.

Personal information: Personally identifiable information.

PII: Personally identifiable information.

PIN: Personal identification number.

PKI: Public key infrastructure.

Plaintext: Unencrypted information.

Policy: Statements, rules or assertions that specify correct or expected behavior.

Practice statement: A formal statement of the practices followed by the parties to an authentication process (e.g., CSP or Verifier). It usually describes the parties' policies and practices and can become legally binding.

Precursor: An observable occurrence or sign that an attacker may be preparing to cause an incident.

Predictability: Enabling reliable assumptions by individuals, owners, and operators about PII and its processing by an information system.

Presentation attack: Presentation to the biometric data capture subsystem with the goal of interfering with the operation of the biometric system.

Presentation attack detection: Automated determination of a presentation attack. A subset of presentation attack determination methods, referred to as liveness detection, involves measurement and analysis of anatomical characteristics or involuntary or voluntary reactions, in order to determine if a biometric sample is being captured from a living Subject present at the point of capture.

Preparedness: The activities to build, sustain, and improve readiness capabilities to prevent, protect against, respond to, and recover from natural or manmade incidents.

Privacy: Protecting personally identifiable information.

Private key: A cryptographic key that must be kept confidential and is used to enable the operation of an asymmetric (public key) cryptographic algorithm. The secret part of an asymmetric key pair that is uniquely associated with an entity.

Privilege escalation: Attackers often need more privileges on a system to get access to more data and system permissions. Once inside, they use techniques to increase their own access privileges, often to the most powerful "administrator" status.

Processing: Operation or set of operations performed upon PII that can include, but is not limited to, the collection, retention, logging, generation, transformation, use, disclosure, transfer, and disposal of PII.

Protect and defend: Identification, analysis, and mitigation of threats to internal IT systems or networks.

Protective DNS: A tool to block employees from visiting potentially malicious domains on the internet.

Protected session: A session wherein messages between two participants are encrypted and integrity is protected using a set of shared secrets called session keys. A protected session is said to be authenticated if, during the session, one participant proves possession of one or more authenticators in addition to the session keys, and if the other party can verify the identity associated with the authenticator(s). If both participants are authenticated, the protected session is said to be mutually authenticated.

Protocol: Technical method.

Pseudonymous identifier: A meaningless but unique number that does not allow the RP to infer anything regarding the Subscriber but which does permit the RP to associate multiple interactions with the Subscriber's claimed identity.

Public key certificate: A digital document issued and digitally signed by the private key of a certificate authority that binds an identifier to a Subscriber to a public key. The certificate indicates that the Subscriber identified in the certificate has sole control and access to the private key.

Public key cryptography: A branch of cryptography in which a cryptographic system or algorithms use two uniquely linked keys: a public key and a private key (a key pair). Asymmetric cryptography, or public key encryption.

Public key encryption: Public key cryptography.

Public key infrastructure: A framework consisting of standards and services to enable secure, encrypted communication and authentication over potentially insecure networks such as the Internet. A framework and services for generating, producing, distributing, controlling, accounting for, and revoking (destroying) public key certificates.

Public key: A cryptographic key that may be widely published and is used to enable the operation of an asymmetric (public key) cryptographic algorithm. The public part of an asymmetric key pair that is uniquely associated with an entity and that may be made public.

R

RaaS: Ransomware as a Service.

Ransomware as a service: A criminal business model used by criminal ransomware software developers in which they lease ransomware in the same way that legitimate software developers lease software as a service (SaaS) products. In this way, regardless of their technical skills, criminals can purchase malware from developers on the dark web. The developers receive a portion of the ransom paid by the victim.

Ransomware: A form of malware designed to block access to a computer system or data, often by encrypting data or programs on systems to extort ransom payments from a victim in exchange for decrypting the information and restoring the victim's access to their system or data.

RDP: Remote Desktop Protocol.

Reauthentication: The process of confirming the Subscriber's continued presence and intent to be authenticated during an extended usage session.

Reconnaissance: The observation stage where criminals assess, from the outside, to identify targets and tactics. They research and select target companies and systems, including identification of vulnerabilities.

Recover: Develop and implement plans to restore any capabilities or services that were impaired due to a cyberattack.

Recovery: The activities after an incident or event to restore essential services and operations in the short and medium term and fully restore all capabilities in the longer term.

Red team exercise: An exercise, reflecting real-world conditions, that is conducted as a simulated attempt by an adversary to attack or exploit vulnerabilities in an organization's information systems.

Red team: A group authorized and organized to emulate a potential adversary's attack or exploitation capabilities against an organization's cybersecurity posture.

Redundancy: Additional or alternative systems, sub-systems, assets, or processes that maintain a degree of overall functionality in case of loss or failure of another system, sub-system, asset, or process.

Registration: Enrollment.

Relying party: An entity that relies upon a Verifier's assertion of a Subscriber's identity, typically to process a transaction or grant access to information or a system.

Remote: An information exchange between network-connected devices where the information cannot be reliably protected end-to-end by a single organization's security controls.

Remote Desktop Protocol: A method which provides a user with the means to connect to another computer over a network connection. It is commonly used by the IT department to remotely fix computer issues. However, it also is a method for ransomware attacks.

Replay attack: An attack in which the attacker is able to replay previously captured messages (between a legitimate Claimant and a Verifier) to masquerade as that Claimant to the Verifier or vice versa.

Replay resistance: The property of an authentication process to resist replay attacks, typically by use of an authenticator output that is valid only for a specific authentication.

Resilience: The ability to adapt to changing conditions and prepare for, withstand, and rapidly recover from disruption.

Respond: Develop and implement action regarding a cyberattack.

Response plan: Incident response plan.

Response: The activities that address the short-term, direct effects of an incident and may also support short-term recovery. In cybersecurity, response encompasses both automated and manual activities.

Risk analysis: The systematic examination of the components and characteristics of risk.

Risk assessment: The product or process which collects information and assigns values to risks for the purpose of informing priorities, developing or comparing courses of action, and informing decision making. The appraisal of the risks facing an entity, asset, system, or network, organizational operations, individuals, geographic area, other organizations, or society, and includes determining the extent to which adverse circumstances or events could result in harmful consequences.

Risk management: The activity of identifying what information requires what level of protection, and implementing and monitoring that protection.

Risk mitigation: Mitigation.

Risk-based data management: A structured approach to managing risks to data and information by which an organization selects and applies appropriate security controls in compliance with policy and commensurate with the sensitivity and value of the data.

Risk: A function of threats, vulnerabilities, the likelihoods, and the potential impact that a particular cyberattack would have.

Rootkit: A set of software tools with administrator-level access privileges installed on an information system and designed to hide the presence of the tools, maintain the access privileges, and conceal the activities conducted by the tools.

RP: Relying party.

S

Salt: A non-secret value used in a cryptographic process, usually to ensure that the results of computations for one instance cannot be reused by an attacker.

Scans: Activity that seeks to access vulnerabilities.

Secret key: A cryptographic key that is used for both encryption and decryption, enabling the operation of a symmetric key cryptography scheme. Also, a cryptographic algorithm that uses a single key (i.e., a secret key) for both encryption of plaintext and decryption of ciphertext.

Secure sockets layer: TLS/SSL.

Securely provision: Conceptualizing, designing, and building secure IT systems, with responsibility for some aspect of the systems' development.

Security automation: The use of information technology in place of manual processes for cyber incident response and management.

Security incident: Incident.

Security patch: Addresses cybersecurity vulnerabilities to protect the system.

Security policy: A rule or set of rules that govern the acceptable use of an organization's information and services to a level of acceptable risk and the means for protecting the organization's information assets. A rule or set of rules applied to an information system to provide security services.

Security program management: Managing information security (e.g., information security) implications within the organization, specific program, or other area of responsibility, to include strategic, personnel, infrastructure, policy enforcement, emergency planning, security awareness, and other resources (e.g., the role of a Chief Information Security Officer).

Session: A persistent interaction between a Subscriber and an endpoint, either an RP or a CSP. A session begins with an authentication event and ends with a session termination event. A session is bound by use of a session secret that the Subscriber's software (a browser, application, or OS) can present to the RP to prove association of the session with the authentication event.

Session hijack attack: An attack in which the attacker is able to insert themselves between a Claimant and a Verifier subsequent to a successful authentication exchange between the latter two parties. The attacker is able to pose as a Subscriber to the Verifier or vice versa to control session data exchange. Sessions between the Claimant and the RP can be similarly compromised.

Shared secret: A secret used in authentication that is known to the Subscriber and the Verifier.

Side-channel attack: An attack enabled by leakage of information from a physical cryptosystem. Characteristics that could be exploited in a side-channel attack include timing, power consumption, and electromagnetic and acoustic emissions.

Signature: A recognizable, distinguishing pattern. Types of signatures: attack signature, digital signature, electronic signature.

Single-factor: A characteristic of an authentication system or an authenticator that requires only one authentication factor (i.e., one of: something you know, something you have, or something you are) for successful authentication.

Single sign-on: An authentication method that allows a user to log in with a single identity to access any of several related, but independent, software systems. True single sign-on allows the user to log in once and access services without re-entering any authentication factors.

Situational awareness: Comprehending information about the current and developing security posture and risks, based on information gathered, observation and analysis, and knowledge or experience. Comprehending the current status and security posture with respect to availability, confidentiality, and integrity of networks, systems, users, and data, as well as projecting future states of these.

Social engineering: An attempt to obtain physical or electronic access to business information by manipulating, fooling or conning people. It often takes the form of a fake phone call from "John in the IT Department" asking for a password to enable him "fix" your computer.

Software assurance and security engineering: Developing and coding new or modified computer applications, software, or specialized utility programs following software assurance best practices.

Software assurance: The level of confidence that software is free from vulnerabilities, either intentionally designed into the software or accidentally inserted at any time during its lifecycle, and that the software functions in the intended manner.

Spam: Electronic junk mail to indiscriminately send unsolicited bulk messages.

Spillage: Data spill, data breach.

Spoof: Using the IP address of another computer or identity of a user to masquerade as a trusted source to gain access to a system. Impersonating, masquerading, piggybacking, and mimicking are forms of spoofing.

Spyware: A form of malware which spies on a user. The aim is to gather information about a person or organization without their knowledge. It may send such information to others without the user's consent and can take over control of a device without the user's knowledge.

SQL: Structured query language.

SSO: Single sign-on.

SSL: TLS/SSL.

State actor: A government which is primarily driven to destroy or disrupt an organization's system or to steal intellectual property and trade secrets for cyberespionage and economic reasons.

Strategic planning and policy development: Applying knowledge of priorities to define an entity.

Structured query language injection attack: A type of cyberattack in which a criminal uses a piece of structured query language code to manipulate a database to obtain access to information.

Subject: A person, organization, device, hardware, network, software, or service.

Subscriber: An individual enrolled in the CSP identity service.

Subscriber account: An account established by the CSP containing information and authenticators registered for each subscriber enrolled in the CSP identity service.

Supervised remote identity proofing: A remote identity proofing process that employs physical, technical and procedural measures that provide sufficient confidence that the remote session can be considered equivalent to a physical, in-person identity proofing process.

Supervisory control and data acquisition: A generic name for a computerized system that is capable of gathering and processing data and applying operational controls to geographically dispersed assets over long distances.

Supply chain attacks: A criminal infiltrates a service supply organization and infects their system with ransomware, often through a seemingly normal software update.

Supply chain risk management: The process of identifying, analyzing, and assessing supply chain risk and accepting, avoiding, transferring or controlling it to an acceptable level considering associated costs and benefits of any actions taken.

Supply chain: A system of organizations, people, activities, information and resources, for creating and moving products including product components and/or services from suppliers through to their customers.

Symmetric cryptography: A branch of cryptography in which a cryptographic system or algorithms use the same secret key (a shared secret key).

Symmetric encryption algorithm: Symmetric cryptography.

Symmetric key: A cryptographic key that is used to perform both the cryptographic operation and its inverse, for example to encrypt plaintext and decrypt ciphertext, or create a message authentication code and to verify the code. Also, a cryptographic algorithm that uses a single key (i.e., a secret key) for both encryption of plaintext and decryption of ciphertext.

Synthetic identity fraud: The use of a combination of personally identifiable information (PII) to fabricate a person or entity in order to commit a dishonest act for personal or financial gain.

System administration: Installing, configuring, troubleshooting, and maintaining server configurations (hardware and software) to ensure their confidentiality, integrity, and availability; also managing accounts, firewalls, and patches; responsibility for access control, passwords, and account creation and administration.

System integrity: The attribute of an information system when it performs its intended function in an unimpaired manner, free from deliberate or inadvertent unauthorized manipulation of the system.

System: An information system.

Systems development: Working on the development phases of the systems development lifecycle.

Systems requirements planning: Consulting with customers to gather and evaluate functional requirements and translates these requirements into technical solutions; providing guidance to customers about applicability of information systems to meet business needs.

Systems security analysis: Conducting the integration/testing, operations, and maintenance of systems security.

Systems security architecture: Developing system concepts and working on the capabilities phases of the systems development lifecycle; translating technology and environmental conditions (e.g., law and regulation) into system and security designs and processes.

T

Tabletop exercise: A discussion-based exercise where personnel meet in a classroom setting or breakout groups and are presented with a scenario to validate the content of plans, procedures, policies, cooperative agreements or other information for managing an incident.

Tailored trustworthy space: A cyberspace environment that provides a user with confidence in its security, using automated mechanisms to ascertain security conditions and adjust the level of security based on the user's context and in the face of an evolving range of threats.

Targets: Applying current knowledge of one or more regions, countries, non-state entities, and/or technologies.

Technology research and development: Conducting technology assessment and integration processes; providing and supporting a prototype capability and/or evaluating its utility.

Test and evaluation: Developing and conducting tests of systems to evaluate compliance with specifications and requirements by applying principles and methods for cost-effective planning, evaluating, verifying, and validating of technical, functional, and performance characteristics (including interoperability) of systems or elements of systems incorporating information technology.

Threat actor: Threat agent.

Threat agent: An individual, group, organization, or government that conducts or has the intent to conduct detrimental activities.

Threat analysis: The detailed evaluation of the characteristics of individual threats. Identifying and assessing the capabilities and activities of cyber criminals or foreign intelligence entities; producing findings to help initialize or support law enforcement and counterintelligence investigations or activities.

Threat assessment: The product or process of identifying or evaluating entities, actions, or occurrences, whether natural or man-made, that have or indicate the potential to harm life, information, operations, and/or property.

Threat: A circumstance or event with the potential to adversely impact organizational operations (including mission, functions, or reputation), organizational assets, individuals, other organizations, through a system via unauthorized access, destruction, disclosure, modification of information, and/or denial of service.

Ticket: In access control, data that authenticates the identity of a client or a service and, together with a temporary encryption key (a session key), forms a credential.

TLS/SSL: Transport Layer Security/Secure Sockets Layer encryption.

Token: Authenticator.

Traffic light protocol: A set of designations employing four colors (red, amber, green, and white) used to ensure that sensitive information is shared with the correct audience.

Transaction: A discrete event between a user and a system that supports a business or programmatic purpose. A digital system may have multiple categories or types of transactions, which may require separate analysis within the overall digital identity risk assessment.

Transport Layer Security/Secure Sockets Layer encryption: A method to encrypt communications between a computer and server, primarily between web browsers and websites.

Trojan horse: A computer program that appears to have a useful function, but also has a hidden and potentially malicious function that evades security mechanisms, sometimes by exploiting legitimate authorizations of a system entity that invokes the program.

Trust anchor: A public or symmetric key that is trusted because it is directly built into hardware or software, or securely provisioned via out-of-band means, rather than because it is vouched for by another trusted entity (e.g. in a public key certificate). A trust anchor may have name or policy constraints limiting its scope.

Two factor authentication: A form of multi-factor authentication.

U

Unauthorized access: Gaining illicit remote or physical access to a system.

Universal Serial Bus: Type of standard cable, connector, and protocol for connecting computers, electronic devices, and power sources.

URL: Uniform resource locator, i.e. "http://website.com/doc.html".

Usability: The extent to which a product can be used by specified users to achieve specified goals with effectiveness, efficiency, and satisfaction in a specified context of use.

USB: Universal Serial Bus.

User: The person who is interacting with a computer or other device.

V

Validation: The process or act of checking and confirming that the evidence and attributes supplied by an Applicant are authentic, accurate and associated with a real-life identity. Specifically, evidence validation is the process or act of checking that presented evidence is authentic, current, and issued from an acceptable source; attribute validation is the process or act of confirming that a set of attributes are accurate and associated with a real-life identity.

Vector: Attack method.

Vector: Method of cyberattack.

Verification: The process or act of confirming that the Applicant holds the claimed identity represented by the validated identity attributes and associated evidence.

Verifier: An entity that verifies the Claimant's identity by verifying the Claimant's possession and control of one or more authenticators using an authentication protocol. To do this, the Verifier needs to confirm the binding of the authenticators with the subscriber account and check that the Subscriber account is active.

Verifier impersonation: Phishing can be one simple example.

Virtual private network: An application which extends a private network across a public network and enables users to send and receive data across shared or public networks as securely as if their computing devices were directly connected to the private network.

Virus: A computer program that can replicate itself, infect a computer without permission or knowledge of the user, and then spread or propagate to another computer.

VPN: Virtual private network.

Vulnerability assessment and management: Conducting assessments of threats and vulnerabilities, determining deviations from acceptable configurations, organization or local policy, assessing the level of risk, and develops and/or recommending appropriate mitigation countermeasures in operational and non-operational situations.

Vulnerability: A weakness in a system, system security procedures, internal controls, or implementation that could be exploited by a criminal to harm an organization.

W

Weakness: A shortcoming or imperfection in software code, design, architecture, or deployment that, under proper conditions, could become a vulnerability or contribute to the introduction of vulnerabilities.

Weaponization: Use of remote access malware and exploits to create a deliverable ransomware payload.

White hat: In contrast to black bat, programmers who seek to access systems to test the system's capabilities, and report vulnerabilities to the organization or authorities for fixing. They often refer to themselves as cybersecurity researchers and seek to be paid fairly for their services. They are not criminals.

White team: A group responsible for refereeing an engagement between a Red Team of mock attackers and a Blue Team of actual defenders of information systems.

Wipe: Electronically erase by completely writing over the entire storage device a sufficient number of times.

Work factor: An estimate of the effort or time needed by a potential adversary, with specified expertise and resources, to overcome a protective measure.

Worm: A self-replicating, self-propagating, self-contained program that uses networking mechanisms to spread itself.

X

XSS: Cross-site scripting.

Z

Zeroize: Overwrite a memory location with data consisting entirely of bits with the value zero (or other random values) so that the data is destroyed and not recoverable. This is often contrasted with deletion methods that merely destroy reference to data within a file system rather than destroying the data itself.

Zero-knowledge password protocol: A password-based authentication protocol that allows a Claimant to authenticate to a Verifier without revealing the password to the Verifier.

Bibliography

CyBOK Version 1.1.0, *The Cyber Security Body of Knowledge*, The
National Cyber Security Centre, (2021),
https://www.cybok.org/media/downloads/CyBOK_v1.1.0.pdf

FATF, *Guidance on Digital Identity*, FATF, (2020), www.fatf-
gafi.org/publications/documents/digital-identity-guidance.html

NIST, *SP 800-63 Digital Identity Guidelines*, National Institute of
Standards and Technology, (2022),
https://pages.nist.gov/800-63-4/sp800-63.html

NIST, *SP 800-63A Enrollment & Identity Proofing*, National Institute
of Standards and Technology, (2023),
https://pages.nist.gov/800-63-4/sp800-63a.html

Acknowledgments

I would like to acknowledge and thank all those who assisted me with this book. I would especially like to thank my good friend and superb lawyer, Robert Carolina, who wrote the excellent, authoritative, and detailed *Law & Regulation* chapter in *The Cyber Security Body of Knowledge*, which chapter is the principal source of the Law and Regulation chapter in this book. I would also like to specifically acknowledge the excellent cited public domain publications of the National Initiative for Cybersecurity Careers and Studies, and the National Institute of Standards and Technology of which I have used significant important portions.

Manufactured by Amazon.ca
Bolton, ON